Wakefield Press

Behind the Veil

In twenty-five years of nursing, Lydia Laube has delivered babies on her knees in New Guinea, tended clinics in dug-out canoes in Papua, worked on a junk in the Hong Kong harbour, served the poor in the slums of Naples and flown with the Australian flying doctor service. She has been marooned by floodwaters in rugged mountains, cut off by cyclones on a tropical island, cast adrift in a disabled boat in a typhoon. None of this prepared her for her experiences as a nurse in Saudi Arabia. She is resting in her home town of Adelaide.

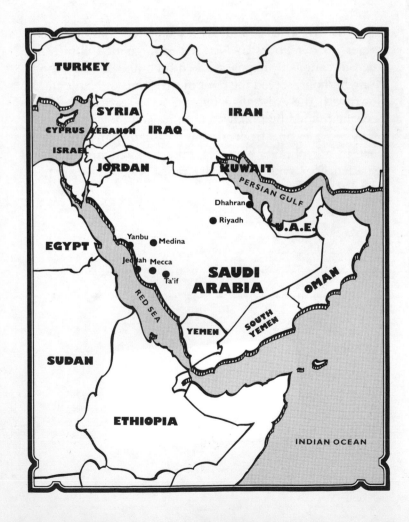

TURKEY

SYRIA

CYPRUS LEBANON IRAQ

ISRAEL

JORDAN

IRAN

KUWAIT

PERSIAN GULF

Dhahran

Riyadh

U.A.E.

EGYPT

Yanbu ● Medina

Jeddah ● Mecca

Ta'if

SAUDI
ARABIA

OMAN

RED SEA

YEMEN

SOUTH
YEMEN

SUDAN

ETHIOPIA

INDIAN OCEAN

Behind the Veil
An Australian nurse in Saudi Arabia

LYDIA LAUBE

Wakefield Press

Wakefield Press
Box 2266
Kent Town
South Australia 5071

First published 1991
Reprinted 1991 (twice), 1992, 1993, 1994.
1995, 1997.

Design by Ann Wojczuk
Cover design by Bill Farr

Printed and bound by Hyde Park Press Pty Ltd,
4 Deacon Avenue, Richmond, South Australia 5033

Cataloguing-in-publication data

Laube, Lydia, 1948-
Behind the Veil:
an Australian nurse in Saudi Arabia
ISBN 1 86254 267 8.
1. Laube, Lydia, 1948-, Journeys.
2. Nurses – Australia – Biography.
3. Saudi Arabia – Description and travel.
I. Title
610.73092

Contents

1 Eyeless in Riyadh

Riyadh airport is magnificent. Designed to represent a traditional Beduin tent, its roof billows high overhead, lofty and cool. Beneath are wonderful gardens and fountains lit by enormous skylights. Just like *Lawrence of Arabia*, I thought, seeing for the first time the Arab's fascination for water and green, growing things.

My appreciation was rudely cut short: the immigration officer, after discovering that I was alone, took my passport and summoned a guard who hurriedly bundled me away from the queue of passengers. The guard, dressed like a policeman, led me to a place labelled 'Women's Room' in Arabic and English. He knocked on the door and gestured to go in. The room was presided over by two large apparitions covered, eyes and all, in black shrouds. I presumed them to be women, only because of the legend on the door. They could have been gorillas in there for all I could see, and they were about the right size.

They opened the door a crack and had a lengthy conversation with the guard. No-one spoke English. They kept asking me questions in Arabic, but eventually the guard got tired of this and went away leaving me in the charge of the women, who shut the door and turned to scrutinise me. I was convinced that I had been arrested: with visions of ghastly prisons before me, I sat down in a comfortable chair and tried deep breathing. The women began to question me again, perhaps thinking that I might have learned to speak Arabic in the short space of time that I had been left in their care. I tried to get through to them that my company representative was waiting to collect me (I sincerely hoped he was).

We soon gave up. As soon as the man had departed and they were behind closed doors, my guards removed their face veils and I discovered that they were Egyptians. Before, in my apprehensive state, it had seemed that I was confronting two large bundles of black cloth. They were covered from head to foot in the full Muslim dress of *purdah*. Even their hands and feet were black, for they were wearing black gloves and socks. They removed their veils by throwing the flap which covered the face up and over the back of the head. Everything else remained covered. At a knock on the door, they could simply drop the flap down again and retire into oblivion. I later discovered that the eye-covering is gauzy and you can see through it dimly but, to somebody new to all this, it was very disconcerting to be speaking to someone without any eyes.

I had learned enough to realise that their questions all pertained to my lack of a husband. I longed for a husband, anybody's, as long as he would take me away from all this. I was in no position to be fussy. And where was that mythical beast, the company representative, who was to have met me at the airport? I worried what would happen if no-one collected me. Would I be sold off as lost property at the next auction, like the bits and pieces people leave on trains and buses in Australia?

I had discovered in my many Asian journeys that to panic or cry is the worst thing to do. It is always best to try to behave as the locals do and throw yourself upon their mercy. So I gave myself up to the will of Allah and practised Eastern calm. I was to do this many times during my sojourn in Saudi Arabia.

2　The desert song

'Nurses wanted for Saudi Arabia.' Where could you go warmer than Arabia, I thought? It was the end of June and I was living in Sydney. I was sitting in my draughty old flat, huddled over an inadequate heater, wearing more clothes than an Eskimo and still cold to the bone, reading the *Sydney Morning Herald*. I could not have been in a more receptive mood. Apart from urging nurses to depart forthwith to warmer climes and take up posts in some romantic desert spot, the advertisement offered a generous tax-free salary and lots of other monetary enticements dear to the heart of an avaricious Capricorn.

I took up the phone and arranged an interview the next day at Alpha Recruiting Agency, which supplied staff to several companies that managed hospitals throughout the Middle East. The firm was looking for senior nurses with management experience and qualifications to work as charge sisters and supervisors in Saudi Arabia. This sounded like me: I am a registered nurse and midwife with tertiary qualifications in nursing management and many years experience, much of it in remote areas of the north and north-west of Australia, New Guinea, Papua and Indonesia. This kind of bush nursing is not for the faint-hearted but, if you survive, it equips you well for just about anything.

During the interview I learned that, although almost all staff are imported from other countries, a nurse wishing to work in Saudi Arabia cannot apply directly to a hospital for a position. The Saudis run their hospitals on a contract basis. They have no qualified Saudi staff, so they hire a company, usually from the UK, Europe or the US, to provide staff and management for them. The company then employs a recruiter to find the staff and deal with the long and difficult business of getting work permits, entry visas and arranging travel. The staff nurses are recruited in large numbers from India, the Philippines, Pakistan, Korea and neighbouring Arab countries such as Egypt, where wages are low and nurses can be hired cheaply. More senior staff are recruited from the west – the UK, US and Australia.

Saudi hospitals mostly belong to the government, either through the Ministry of Health (MOH) or the Ministry of Defence (MODA). There are also some private hospitals owned by doctors or businessmen. The recruiters find suitable people and send their credentials to the managing company, which gives them to the hospital's owner for approval. If this is granted, a work permit and entry visa are obtained from the government. All being well, the person is accepted, hired, and toddles out to Saudi Arabia to repent this folly at leisure.

I must have passed the initial scrutiny, as Alpha invited me to attend a seminar on Saudi Arabia at the Hilton Hotel. There were slides, films, photos and discussion time. Naturally, all aspects of life in Saudi Arabia for an expatriate worker were presented in a glowing light.

A fortnight later the recruiter rang me to see if I was willing to be submitted for a post as a nursing supervisor at the King Fahid Hospital at Medina, a five hundred bed government hospital belonging to the Ministry of Health and managed by a company called Omega Health Services. I asked for further details and was told that Medina was remote and considered a hardship posting, and that most of its patients were Beduin; that was all she knew about it, as Alpha had not sent anyone to Medina before.

I agreed to accept the position if approval was granted, thinking that in the meantime I would find out more about conditions there. If I did not like the sound of it, I could always withdraw my application. Having spent much time in isolated areas, I did not consider Medina's remoteness a drawback. I took myself off to the library to do some research, but there was little information on modern Saudi Arabia, and no tourist guides, because no tourists are permitted – the only foreigners allowed into the country are those who go with a work permit and an employer's sponsorship, or Muslims making the holy pilgrimage. Most books I found were either historical or autobiographies of explorers: they were interesting, but I wanted to know what to expect, what it would be like to work there now, what I needed to take with me, and what would be available locally. I read all I could, but found only vague and passing references to Medina. It is the second holy city of Islam, after Mecca, and therefore forbidden to non-Muslims, so that only members of the faith could have written about it. I had heard of Mecca, but I had to confess ignorance of Medina. I had been told that the hospital was outside the walls of the city. Now I understood why. A great many of the staff would be non-Muslim.

During the next couple of weeks I was hounded by the recruiters with lists of what I had to do and provide to prove my suitability for admission to Saudi Arabia. (In retrospect I reckon that all you need is an advanced case of insanity.) The progress of my application was extremely slow. All the originals of my qualifications had to be sent to the Saudi Ambassador in Canberra, to be certified, before copies could be sent to the MOH in Saudi. The recruiter's word was not good enough, apparently, but now, with my first-hand knowledge of the MOH, I believe that I could have sent them my car registration, or the cat's breeding papers, and they probably would not have known the difference.

I also had to send my birth certificate, passport, health documents, medical certificates, X-rays and the results of many tests. Of prime importance was an AIDS Clearance Certificate, followed by similar verification that I was not infected with VD, Hepatitis B, or any other communicable nasties. For this supplement to my eligibility I had to front the local public hospital's VD clinic, an experience previously denied me by the kind fates and not one I would gladly line up for again.

In the outpatients department I entered a long corridor full of people seated on benches against the wall, under the merciless glare of fluorescent lights (no skulking anonymously here). From an end room, a formidable female bellowed down the line, 'Laube, AIDS test!' I cringed to my feet and sidled past the line of frankly curious faces.

Sister took some blood for tests and an apologetic Indian doctor filled out a form about my personal life. He knew that I was only having the tests as a visa requirement.

'I'm so sorry, Sister, but I have to ask you this. Are you a prostitute?' And on it went.

Eventually all the required forms, certificates, tests,

references, qualifications, verifications and other paper work were despatched by the recruiters. Now all I had to do was wait for approval from MOH – all the documentation went to their headquarters in Riyadh – and for a working visa to enter the country. The second did not automatically follow the first, I learned to my frustration.

In the meantime I got the necessary inoculations and vaccinations. They were not taking any chances. The list included almost every serum known: polio, hepatitis, meningitis, typhoid, tetanus and cholera.

During this time the Australian Nursing Federation issued a statement in the national papers warning nurses against going to Saudi Arabia to work. There had been complaints about conditions and the way nurses had been treated by some of the companies that employed staff. The warning was prompted by the publicity given to the case of an Australian nurse who had been caught drinking alcohol (forbidden in Saudi) and sentenced to a flogging and a prison sentence. At the last moment, she had been given a reprieve and deported.

Later, in Saudi, I was told about two British nurses working in Taif who had missed the company bus when out shopping and had accepted a lift from two young Saudis in a car. They were intercepted by the police before they got to the hospital, arrested, charged with adultery – which is defined as any type of intercourse between unmarried persons – and thrown into prison. Two days later they were deported with 'prostitute' stamped in their passports. They were lucky the full extent of the law against adultery had not been invoked.

When I enquired, the Federation said that if I was really determined to go I must make sure that the contract I was offered was in order before I signed it. My twelve-month contract seemed to be all right, so I did not change my mind. If my visa was granted, I would go. (After all, it was still cold in Sydney!)

The recruiters eventually managed to obtain some information from Omega Health Services about conditions at the hospital, and they sent me some material: 'Living and working at King Fahid Hospital, Medina, will not be a problem for the non-Muslim, as although the city of Medina is forbidden to them, there are substantial shopping and recreational facilities outside the walls and the hospital compound is an enclave of cosmopolitan living where the expatriate may live in the same manner as in his or her own country.'

I learned from the brochure that there was a large recreational facility with a swimming pool in the compound and that I would be able to indulge in all kinds of activities outside the compound, including horse riding. With visions of myself galloping over the desert sands on a fabulous Arabian thoroughbred, I duly packed my jodhpurs and riding boots.

3 White-knuckle flying

There was still no word of my visa. The date I had been given to take up my appointment in Medina was 7 September and it was already early August.

In mid August the phone call came. My visa had been granted. I flew into frenzied activity, resigned from the hospital, sold my car, rented my flat, fostered the cat, stored my belongings and packed my suitcases. It had taken two months from the first interview to the last locking of the suitcases.

I am disgustingly healthy and rarely catch a bug, but perhaps because of the stresses and strains of the last two weeks, I had succumbed to a virus that had developed into bronchitis. Having a deadline to meet, I had not had time to take to my bed, much as I would have liked to, but had pushed on. I flew to Adelaide to spend a couple of days with my family, who were in some trepidation over my latest adventure. Arriving at my mother's house and once again safe in the bosom of my kin, I fell straight into bed and stayed there for two days, letting my mother cosset me. She was convinced, I think, that these would be her last motherly ministrations and that I was departing for a fearful fate in a God-forsaken country.

By 'D' day, 5 September, I was improving. Being a nurse of the old school, where it was a mortal sin to be late, and being ill was no excuse for failing to front (you needed to be in a coma to get any time off), it did not occur to me that I should delay my departure.

Escorted by the family, farewelled tearfully by a mother sure that she would never see me again, and fortified by a large brandy thoughtfully provided by my brother, I boarded a Singapore Airlines flight for Saudi Arabia.

The flight was a good one by my standards, and I am the president of the White-knuckle Flyers Club. The meals and service were excellent, but the film was a sad saga about a woman trying to return, against impossible odds, to her home town – an omen? I could have done with a side-splitting comedy.

I arrived in Singapore several hours later, in the early evening. The flight to Bahrain did not depart until ten o'clock the next night, so a stopover had been booked for me at a hotel. Although I had been to Singapore several times, this was my first visit to Changi Airport, and I was very impressed. It is huge, but superefficient, and I had a very speedy trip through customs, thanks, no doubt, to my Good Little Woman's Outfit. This is the uniform I always don for arrivals and departures in foreign countries. It is designed to convince the world's officialdom of my extreme respectability, and consists of a thoroughly staid, housewifely skirt and blouse with sensible shoes. I always pray fervently that on the way to the airport I never meet anyone I am trying to impress, but I consider it worth the risk. It avoids potential problems in countries that have a strong suspicion of decadent westerners, especially those in jeans or mod clothes.

I was met at the airport and taken to the Crown Prince Hotel by car. On arrival I was told that there were no more regular rooms available but that, if I had no objection, I would have to make do with a suite. I said I would force myself, or words to that effect, and was ushered into this little place to rest my weary head. It was the last gasp in luxury. It had a sauna and spa, sitting-room, dressing-room, a three-roomed bathroom, two toilets, a foyer and conference-room and the usual bedroom. It was so big I almost needed a tracker to help me find my way out. The whole place was festooned with orchids, as if they were expecting royalty rather than a slightly wilted nurse in sensible shoes.

I did enjoy the gorgeous chandeliers, glittering marble and the gold-plated taps. For the occupant's use there were dressing-gowns, kimonos, slippers, hair-dryers, bubble bath – everything you might need.

The next day, after a trip to my favourite Singapore shopping haunts, I headed for the best place in town: the Long Bar at Raffles. Here I downed liberal quantities of their speciality, the Singapore Sling, getting what would be my last taste of freedom and alcohol for a long time.

4 Behind the veil

At ten o'clock I boarded Singapore Airlines flight to Bahrain, via Male in the Maldive Islands. A cyclone was raging across the top of northern India, and we flew through the edge of it, suffering thunderstorms, bolts of lightning and all. There was a loud bang and the plane dropped like a stone, straight down for thousands of feet. It felt like a bomb had exploded. Panic erupted, drinks flew to the roof, and there was chaos until the hostesses got the message through that it had been an airpocket, that we had been victims of the weather, not a terrorist attack. They dished out therapeutic shots of brandy and champagne until everyone settled down again. I vowed never to set foot in another plane, if I should only be lucky enough to get out of this one alive.

We reached Bahrain after an interminable, nervewracking and sleepless night. It was a shock to find myself suddenly in the Arab world at three in the morning. The airport was full of men in long white nighties with red checked cloths draped over their heads; there was not a woman in sight. I felt very self-conscious, but I played this to my advantage. I asked the airline to find me somewhere to sleep until the plane left for Saudi Arabia. At first I was told there was nowhere, but when I replied that I would sleep right there, on the airport bench, I was very quickly provided with a voucher for a hotel room.

Bahrain is, by Saudi Arabian standards, very liberated. Foreign women may wear western dress as long as it is modest – long sleeves and trousers, loose-fitting clothes that do not show the form – but the attitude towards women has not changed. The first words spoken to me in my first Arab country were, 'Where is your husband?'

When I said that I did not have one of those articles at present about my person, the immigration official looked at me as though I had come from another planet. Again, at customs I was asked, 'Where is your husband?' This time when I replied that I did not have a husband, the customs man promptly tried to chat me up. 'Then I will come to visit you.' He leered at me, in what he meant to be an inviting manner. I gave him a sickly smile.

I was driven to my hotel by a reluctant airport driver, who obviously disapproved of my being out unaccompanied at four in the morning. It was five before I was in my room, which was not a patch on my previous night's glory, but by this time I could have slept on a barbed-wire fence.

At half past eight I was once more on my way back to the airport. Now, in the daylight, I could see Bahrain. I am not sure what I expected the Middle East to look like. I had only vague ideas, formed from films such as *Beau Geste*, of romantic oases surrounded by waving palm trees, sand dunes with turreted forts nestling among them. Bahrain was very disappointing. In the brilliant glare of the sun, the buildings were square, new, and dazzling white. There was no colour anywhere except for the occasional green of a palm tree, which could not make much of a statement against these odds.

I had been warned by the recruiter to dress suitably before getting on the plane to Saudi (I was flying on Saudia, Saudi Arabia's national airline), so I was wearing a voluminous long black skirt, and a long-sleeved, high-necked overshirt that covered and occluded my hips. I felt foolish and very uncomfortable in the intense heat. There was another European woman (obviously a very proper person) on the transport, complete with the obligatory husband. They were schoolteachers returning to Saudi after leave, and she was wearing a very smart suit. Being an old hand at the game she had her *abeya* – the all-enveloping black shroud – in her bag, ready to put on before the plane touched down.

By now my ears were aching and I had gone somewhat deaf. I was still suffering from an infection, and I was groggy from lack of sleep. Only my adrenalin kept me going. The flight into Saudi Arabia and Riyadh, the capital, was only an hour across the Arabian Gulf. As the plane taxied down the runway out of Bahrain, a wonderful, resonant male voice came over the intercom, intoning in Arabic the prayer for travellers. I did not know whether to be reassured that I was being taken care of, or terrified that we were literally flying on a wing and a prayer.

Overhead, in the centre of the plane, was a round object, like a big compass. Its hand pointed at all times to Mecca, so that the faithful knew in which direction to turn when praying.

At that time the Iranians were firing missiles at aircraft flying over the Arabian Gulf, but luckily their aim was off that day and all I had to contend with was the now minor terror of a bumpy ride.

From the air Riyadh appeared to be another all-white

city, surrounded by open country of red earth and sand dunes. As we came in lower, though, the monotonous whites gave way to the tawny glow of the old mud brick houses. I later heard Riyadh described as the city with the colour of the desert.

We sat waiting in the 'Women's Room', the ladies in fascinated study of this awful woman who had been apprehended wandering at large, and I, outwardly calm but inwardly petrified. I believed I had been arrested, and I suppose in a way I had been, for I was certainly in custody. An hour passed. Every now and then an official would knock at the door and, after dropping their veils over their faces, the ladies would open it a crack and talk to him. Now that I had seen their faces, I could have told them that if the object of this exercise was to prevent an attack of lust at the sight of their countenances, they need not have bothered. (I had progressed from feeling testy to downright nasty.)

After more than two hours of this nerve-racking treatment, the door was opened, and I was led out to customs to collect my baggage. I was then handed over to the company representative, who had been there trying to claim me. This poor man, who was Sudanese and spoke beautiful Oxford English, was embarrassed by my presence and could not get rid of me fast enough. He galloped me along endless miles of corridors, over interminable shiny floors trying to keep five paces ahead of me, as is seemly. The faster I went, trying to catch up with him, the faster he went trying to keep a proper distance between us.

Eventually we reached the domestic counter for my flight to Medina where I was once again the only woman in a large crowd of men. At home, in a former life, this would have caused me no concern, but I had already grown used to feeling uncomfortable. Arabs do not queue. There was just a wild, pushing throng, heaving and shoving to reach the counter. My Sudanese escort fought his way into the crowd and, in time, came out holding my boarding pass. He rushed me to the gate of the departure lounge, saw me inside, and left.

I had been warned that flights are only called in Arabic so, when an hour later there was an announcement that prompted everyone to rise and go to the door, I followed them. I hoped it was Medina we were all heading for. Another rugby scrum ensued, with everyone pushing and shoving to get on the plane. I just tagged along in the rear trying to avoid most of the battering. This was a Saudia domestic flight. The hostesses were Arabic but recruited from countries outside Saudi Arabia; Saudi girls would not be permitted to do that sort of work.

The air was clear apart from a sand haze that shrouded everything in a beige film. I had heard horror stories of sand storms and aeroplanes, but my neighbour, an Egyptian working for an oil company in Saudi Arabia, told me that flying was invariably rough here, because of the great heat rising off the desert. He said that the haze was normal too, caused by drifting sands. Anyway, we enjoyed the blessings of the traveller's prayer at take-off, and I consoled myself that all contingencies had been taken care of.

Refreshments were served shortly and they consisted of what appeared to be a glass of milk, some dates and a cup of coffee. Now I am allergic to certain foods, and coffee and dates are among them, and I really dislike milk. But I was desperate for a drink, so I took a long swig from the glass. My whole face puckered, and I felt green all over. It was the local delicacy: fermented camel's milk. I thought it was revolting.

At last I had my first glimpse of Medina. From the air it was a mass of square whitish buildings surrounded by desert, its only outstanding feature the big green dome of the Great Mosque of The Prophet. I peeked at this surreptitiously, wondering if it was blasphemous for my infidel eyes to gaze upon it. It was now four in the afternoon, and I was on the point of exhaustion, dehydrated, starving and, thanks to my ear infection, disorientated and deaf. I had been up all night, flown through some terrifying weather, been detained, subjected to enormous stress, and had no sustenance for what seemed like days. And I was alone in an alien culture. In trepidation I stepped down from the plane.

5 Forbidden city

At least there were no arrival formalities in Medina, just the business of collecting your luggage and being collected (which I fervently prayed I was going to be). I felt very conspicuous. In the throng of passengers I was the only European and the only woman not submerged and wrapped in black. At the end of the reception area was a large crowd of men in white robes and red checked head-dresses waiting to meet passengers. From among this crowd emerged a tall, thin, middle-aged man, wearing western dress. He approached me, asked if I was Miss Laube and introduced himself as Len Fitch, the chief nursing officer of King Fahid Hospital. I judged by his accent that he was a Scot. He was accompanied by a scrawny Arab. Mustafa was the driver, and a more morose and surly individual would be hard to find. We were not introduced: that would have been unthinkable. Mustafa was a Bedu, not long out of the desert and not at all familiar with western ways. He always appeared to thoroughly disapprove of us. Driving was one of the few things the Bedu would consider doing as a job. They saw it as macho and not demeaning, as manual labour was, and they certainly drove in the most macho way possible.

We went to the carpark. Mustafa did not help with my luggage, so Len Fitch and I struggled with my two bags across sizzling concrete in the blazing sun, while Mustafa sauntered ahead. He could have brought the transport to the door, but he obviously did not care to. Mustafa had no English, but I got the distinct impression that, even if he had, Len Fitch would not have remonstrated with him.

We set off on the seventeen kilometre trip to the hospital. They drive on the right-hand side of the road in Saudi Arabia, or they are supposed to, but the truth is that they drive anywhere they feel like. The vehicle was a small Japanese mini-bus, the company's only transport, apart from the chief administrator's car, which we lesser mortals rarely saw. The airconditioning was not working, and the heat was tremendous. Togged as I was in my neck-to-toe stuff, I felt awful. The view along the way was depressing and my heart sank. It looked like a never-ending rubbish tip: high cyclone fences lined the roadway, and litter was blown up against them, one or two feet high all the way. There was nothing to break the monotonous sight of the brown desert and the hot, dusty road except occasional white or beige mud brick houses, some of them little more than hovels or sheds. They were all similar square boxes with flat roofs. There was no colour anywhere, no green, no trees, no grass or gardens, some contrast for one who had just come from the early spring of southern Australia.

We went nowhere near Medina, as the road does a wide circle around it to protect it from contamination by infidels. I was never to learn any more about it than I could glean from descriptions given by Muslim friends. It is a major crime for a non-Muslim to enter the holy city of Medina, which is why the only large government hospital in the district is 'without the walls' – almost all the medical and nursing staff are foreigners, and a large number of them are infidels.

We passed through a small village of depressing squalor, a cluster of squat, square buildings surrounded by litter and old cars. No gardens, fences or livestock were anywhere to be seen. I had imagined the country-side would be hot and dry but vividly scenic, with quantities of clean and yellow sand and an odd camel. I was accordingly extremely disenchanted, and my escort did nothing to elevate my mood. After a little more conversation I had worked out that he must be the matron, or director of nursing, of the hospital. Ignorant of British terms, I had not known what a chief nursing officer did. In the half hour that it took to reach our destination, he enlightened me. I gathered that he was not happy in the service. I was now, he said, a paid slave of the king and could expect to be treated accordingly. I would be living like a prisoner, and the life of a female worker was especially hard.

Not long after he had passed on these words of encouragement, we arrived at the hospital gates. They were barred by a boom that was raised for us by an armed and uniformed guard. So far he was right about the prison. The hospital was a huge six-storey concrete block and behind it the housing, stretching as far as you could see, was similar. All the roads and the areas surrounding the buildings were made of concrete: there were acres of it, baking hot, and burning your eyes, rolling away to infinity.

The female housing, or *harem*, was on one side of the compound enclosed by a wall. The word 'harem' means both 'woman' and 'forbidden'. There was only one entrance, through a gateway where an armed guard was stationed in a sentry box, twenty-four hours a day.

My skin fried through the layers of clothing. With the

aid of Len Fitch, I managed to drag my luggage up three flights of stairs to my accommodation. Len Fitch beat a hasty retreat at the door, as he had special dispensation, in his capacity as CNO, to see me as far as that. He told me that he would wait outside to take me to the hospital, and that I must cover my hair with a scarf. Imagine my embarrassment to discover that I had committed a profound indiscretion. I had been sashaying about in a state of serious undress, the equivalent of walking topless down a main street at home.

Throwing my bags inside the door, I rummaged through them until I found a head scarf. Outside once more, I set off at a brisk walk with Len Fitch towards the hospital. Mustafa and the transport had disappeared. The heat was intense, and it took ten minutes hurrying along searing concrete footpaths to reach the front entrance. Beside the paths and between the buildings there was nothing but hard sandy ground; no grass or plants grew here.

I was taken to meet the chief administrator, Roger Pearce, who was the head of the company at the hospital, a short, chubby, elderly South African. Then I was set to filling out forms and completing other formalities. So far I had not been offered a drink, a wash, or a rest and, apart from my brief flirtation with the fermented camel's milk, I had had no nourishment since breakfast in Bahrain. I was walked around the hospital, introduced to a stream of people and given much and varied information, none of which I absorbed. At half past five, when the company staff finished work, I was released, being told to report again at seven the next morning.

I tottered outside and was confronted by the concrete jungle. It took me a while to find my way back to my quarters, as there were no distinguishing features by which to navigate my way, but at last I made it and set about investigating the place. The accommodation blocks had been built at the same time as the hospital and so were only seven years old, but they had obviously had a very hard life in that time.

I collapsed into a chair, surveyed my situation and reviewed my day. What a terrible reception I had received. It had not seemed to occur to anyone that I had been travelling for two days and should have been left to rest. Finding myself momentarily alone with the first friendly face I had encountered, I had asked for a drink of water. Even that had not been easy. The tap water is not drinkable, and the only water available is from bottles. There were no tea breaks. Drinks had to be sneaked behind closed doors and doors could not be closed unless the occupants of the room were of the same sex. I was, however, given a surreptitious sip of water.

Now the impact of what I had got myself into hit me. It was stultifyingly hot in the sitting-room. I got up, step-ping over the scattered remains of a large dead bird and turned on the airconditioner. Nothing happened. No amount of coaxing would persuade it to work.

The rest of the flat was large and sparsely furnished. The floors were concrete with no coverings, the ceilings ten feet high, there were large windows without curtains, and the entire place was filthy. The decorations could only be described as institutional (and that was doing them a kindness). There was a massive sitting-room rather like a basketball stadium, which was adorned by an old brown couch with chrome legs and arms, a laminex kitchen table and five wooden chairs in various stages of decomposition. In the corner, a phone sat forlornly on the floor. Off from the sitting-room was a kitchen with grease running down the walls, battered and grubby cupboards and bench-tops, and a fridge and stove, neither of which worked. Along a wide corridor from the sitting-room were four small bedrooms with a bathroom between each. The bathrooms were nightmarish, and the bedrooms had only a few derelict pieces of furniture between the lot of them.

I selected the 'best' bedroom, the only room with a working airconditioner in the entire flat, which had a light. Its total furnishings consisted of a bed and wardrobe, both bearing the scars of previous abuse. There were no curtains, bed-linen, towels, pillows, or crockery and cutlery. I had been promised my own fully equipped flat, including radio, television and video. I had made it a condition of my employment that I should not have to share, but Len Fitch had told me that as soon as other staff arrived they would be put in with me, and this flat's capacity was four. This was the first time I was disillusioned by the company's broken promises, but it was not to be the last.

Further inspection revealed that there were only two lights that worked, mainly because there were no bulbs in the fittings; only one of the toilets flushed and that in a half-hearted way – water ran noisily down it all the time – and there was no hot water.

I had been told that the only other western women in the compound lived in the next door flat and that if I wanted anything I should ask them. I rang their bell to ask how I could get something to eat and drink. The door was opened by a large woman who resembled an unmade bed. She was late middle age by vintage and, by accent, I took her to be French. She said she was going to the compound shop shortly and would take me along. Apparently meals were my responsibility when I was off duty. So much for the full board. I went with her to the shop across the compound, very conscious of my uncovered state. All the other women I saw wore *abeyas* with long, black scarves wrapped around their heads and necks. I had not been told to expect this, only that I would have to wear long skirts and sleeves. *Abeyas* and head coverings had not been mentioned. I felt half-dressed, even though I was ridiculously well covered for such a hot day (or a cold one for that matter).

The large French lady, who said she was a nursing supervisor and that her name was Jolie, did nothing to brighten my day. She told me that this was 'a terreebla place' and she was 'so confused'. The shop was another disappointment. My fears that I might starve increased. I found some camel's milk cheese, fruit and a large bottle of mineral water, but nothing else I could eat that did not require cooking or refrigeration, facilities for which I had none. I asked the French woman if her flat had some utensils I could borrow, but she said that they only had enough for themselves, so I ate with my fingers and drank out of the bottle. It seemed pretty good to me.

I had sent on ahead three suitcases containing a few basics such as a towel, two sheets, a pillow, cup, saucer, plate and some eating tools, as the recruiter had said that, although the flat provided would be fully equipped, it was best to take a few basics. My contract stated that I was allowed fifty kilograms in excess of the allowance and that I would be reimbursed for the cost of sending it, but I am still waiting. This baggage should have been at the airport when I arrived, but Len Fitch had shown no inclination to enquire after it, so I had to manage without. By now I was long past caring. All I wanted to do was fall on the bed and sleep.

6 Barely possible

The mattress looked far from inviting in its naked and grubby state, so I spread some of my more voluminous clothing over it, rolled up some more as a pillow and, as there were no curtains, undressed in the dark and lay me down to sleep. But this was not to be. There was a huge spotlight shining right in the window and directly on my face. This housing block was on the edge of the compound and around the compound boundary was a high stone wall, with big spotlights along it at short intervals. It looked just like a concentration camp. I got up to find something to hang over the window, but all possible drapes had already been called into commission as bedclothes. There was nothing else for it but to move the bed out of the light, which I did with no small effort as it seemed to have been constructed from two inch floor boards and weighed a ton. Back on the bed once again, I discovered that after a while it was very cold with the airconditioner on. I got up again to turn it off, but I was soon sweltering. I got out of bed again, this time to investigate the contents of my suitcases for blanket substitutes. Finally, having covered myself with more of my clothes, I fell asleep and slept very badly, until I was woken at dawn by the call to prayer from the compound mosque.

By morning I was feeling ill with earache, a sore chest

and a cough. At half past five I had a cold shower and drip dried, for I had no towel. About to step back into my room, I encountered my first setback for the day. The door had locked behind me and I had no key. As this flat was meant for communal use, each bedroom's door locked automatically when it closed, which it had done, firmly and irrevocably, behind me. Not being in the habit of locking my bedroom when I go to the bathroom, it had not occurred to me to take a key with me. I had, in fact, nothing with me.

I found myself locked out of my bedroom and stark naked. In a country where it is a mortal sin to expose your hair, I had to try and find help. Fortunately there was a phone in the sitting-room, but to make it past the uncurtained windows I had to scuttle along on all fours, up the corridor and across the sitting-room to the corner where, scrunched down out of sight, I dialled at random trying to find a switchboard. There was no directory with the phone. Eventually I hit the jackpot. A male voice answered in Arabic. I asked for the chief nurse, the only person I could remember. He replied in a stream of Arabic. I persisted but could not make him understand, so I said, 'English! Get someone who speaks English.' He hung up, but I was not having that as he was my only link with the outside world. I dialled again and continued where I had left off. This time he connected me to a number that was answered by another man speaking Arabic, who also hung up when he discovered he could not understand me. Later I learned that this is the usual practice. The phone was a continual source of frustration to me. None of the telephonists spoke anything but Arabic, and although there were only a few Europeans in the hospital, there were a great many Asians, among whom the *lingua franca* was English. The

29

telephonists' attitude was, if you could not speak Arabic, it was tough toenails for you. No-one made any attempt to find someone who could understand but dismissed you as unworthy of their attention and promptly hung up.

I have always been proud of my perseverance, but there comes a stage when I admit that there is no point in pursuing a matter. After half an hour of repeated rejections, I decided to desist from furthering a friendship with the telephonist. There was only one other possible solution and that was to seek help from my neighbours. So far my encounter with them had not inspired any great confidence in their generosity, but I had no other option.

Not wanting to give them the novel experience of opening their door at the crack of dawn to behold a naked woman, I toured the flat (via hands and knees) to find some cover. There was absolutely nothing: no curtains or cushions, not even a piece of newspaper. At least I was in the strictly segregated female housing. So, leaving my front door open, I dashed across the corridor, rang their bell, dashed back and retreated behind my door, which I left open a crack.

The door was opened by a woman I had not seen before. This one had an Irish accent, and it was obvious that I had woken her from sleep. With just my eyes and nose showing around the edge of the door, I shouted across the way. She promptly found me a short cotton dressing-gown and, passing it around the door, went off to phone the housing supervisor. I sat down to wait and in the fullness of time there was a knock on the door. I opened it carefully and continued to stand half behind it as a Saudi with a bunch of keys came in, leaving the door open and his chaperone, one of the guards from the harem gate, outside looking in. The poor man looked thunderstruck at my appearance: I might as well have been wearing the seven veils and doing the dance of Salome with a rose between my teeth. Only later did I fully understand the seriousness of this situation.

At last a key was found that opened the door and, with tremendous relief, I was admitted to my clothes.

7 Uniform disaster

It wasn't long before I discovered that I should have brought my own uniforms. The recruiter had told me that they would be provided on site, but the hospital and the company administrator denied any knowledge of this, and I had to try to find something to wear to work. A pair of slacks and a big, loose shirt were all I could find that were in any way suitable. My duty shoes were in my missing suitcases so I had to wear a pair of sandals which, because my feet had swollen with the heat, were too tight and hurt when I walked.

In this attire, and the essential head scarf, I went off to report for duty. I looked horrible. And I felt worse, physically and mentally. I have always taken pride in my professional appearance and have at all times gone on duty in an immaculate uniform, but here I was, reporting for my first day in a new hospital, wearing navy, creased slacks, with a bright, electric blue shirt hanging untidily over them, a multi-coloured head scarf and brown strappy sandals.

Outside, the hot air assaulted me as soon as I stepped from the building. It was even more of a shock after a night spent in too cold airconditioning. I felt very despondent and I wanted desperately to go home. Then I remembered that I no longer had one.

With some effort I found the chief nurse's office – the

hospital was a maze of unfamiliarity – and I put my disenchantment to Len Fitch. I told him that I did not think it was even worthwhile for me to unpack. He said, 'It's up to you.' He could not have cared if I went or stayed. I would have thought that it was his job, as chief nurse, to concern himself with how his staff felt and to make sure that he did all he could to help them adjust. A cup of tea on arrival would have been a good start. That's not the way I would do it, I thought, never dreaming that one day I would end up doing his job.

All that occupied my mind was the thought of getting out at the first opportunity. Len Fitch launched another broadside at me with the information that he was expecting more female company staff very soon, and that I would have to share my flat when they arrived, as MOH had allocated very little housing to the company. I had already learned that the Filipino nurses lived as many as four to a room, sixteen to a flat the same size as mine. For someone who has lived alone by choice for years, this was difficult to accept.

I went to see the administrator and told him that I had been promised single, self-contained accommodation and if this condition was not met I would go home. After a great deal of argument and persuasion, he agreed to give me my own flat when one became available, but said that up until now single women had always been put in shared housing. I began to realise that the hospital and conditions described to me by the recruiter were a figment of someone's imagination. The place I had arrived at in no way resembled the place I had been told about. The contract I had been so careful to check, as advised by the ANF, was worthless. What use is a contract if the company chooses to ignore it and there is no authority to complain to? For the first time in my life I knew what it meant to feel powerless to control my life.

I felt angry and frustrated. I had been conned, and I was helpless to do anything about it. Even if I decided to leave, it could be weeks, I had been told, before I could get out: there was an exit visa to arrange and that is not easy. I would leave at their leisure unless they wanted to deport me, and then they could evict me at once.

After more argument, I managed to convince the administrator that I meant business and that he had to give me my rights. We agreed that I would stay where I was living (camped is more the word) until a smaller, single flat could be found for me, and that in the meantime I would not have to share my accommodation. Roger Pearce also agreed to try to locate my missing suitcases, to get me a uniform, and to have some of the broken furniture in the flat fixed. I was to discover that he was big on promises and short on delivery. He appeared to be a strange man who seemed to have a lot of trouble understanding what I was talking about. I had to repeat over and over the details about my missing suitcases, for example, and I still don't think he absorbed the fact that I had sent them on ahead. He seemed to think I had lost the ones with which I was travelling. I decided he was a bit dense and wondered gloomily, if this was the way of the chief administrator, how the hospital would be run. He was supposed to administer the hospital under the guidance of the hospital director, a Saudi, but it did not exactly work that way. The hospital director interfered in everything, and Roger was too weak to fight him. What saved the enterprise from being a total shambles was that Roger had a very capable deputy, a Welshman aptly named Paul Sharp, who gave every indication of regularly consuming quantities of razor blades for breakfast.

I spent an endless morning of incredible boredom: filling out yet more forms and being photographed for my identity badge and resident's permit, both of which had to be carried the whole time. Then I was paraded through a never-ending succession of offices, and introduced to scores more people.

At one o'clock I was handed over to one of the Filipino sisters who took me to lunch in the dining-room. This was a big area, divided down the centre by a long, floor-to-ceiling curtain that segregated males and females. Finally I had my first meal in the kingdom. Was it only yesterday morning that I had eaten breakfast in Bahrain?

The time allowed for lunch was an hour, so after eating I navigated my way back to my flat. It was much too hot to stay in the sitting-room without an air-conditioner, so I lay down on my bed and fell fast asleep.

After lunch the assistant chief nurse, Sister Fatma, took me to the stores department to get a uniform. Sister Fatma was a Palestinian of mammoth proportions, who dressed in a flowing robe that came from her shoulders, covered her arms to the wrist and obliterated her form completely, stopping just a few inches from the ground. Her head and neck were swathed in a series of scarves and wrappings, just leaving exposed that bit of her face from above her eyebrows to beneath her chin to delight the world. She berated the nurses non-stop at full volume and had them all terrified. She eyed me with a great deal of suspicion, decadent infidel that I was. I was quite prepared to join the nurses and be terrified of her too. She swept into the store-room and shouted at the Saudi storeman in Arabic, which ensured that he did not want to part with a uniform for me and that it took three-quarters of an hour of arguing (them, not me) in a steaming room before he grudgingly threw her a pair of pants and a jacket. These storemen did not want to give anything to anyone but preferred to keep goods in neat piles on their shelves. The answer I was to get, time after time, when I was pleading for essential supplies for the wards was, 'But if I give it to you, I shall have none left here.' He was also making the point that I belonged to the company and that they should get me a uniform – his stock was for Ministry of Health staff – and he was right.

At this stage any uniform was better than none. I went to the female change room in outpatients and tried it on. It was constructed of something strongly resembling white canvas and was made for the figure of the assistant chief nurse. The label said it was made in Egypt and was a small size. With the aid of a couple of large safety pins I anchored the trousers, rolling them up a few times at the feet, so that I could walk without taking a nose dive. The jacket fitted me like a Weeties box, with enough room for me and a couple of friends. It had a high mandarin collar and fell way down over my hips, but only had sleeves to the elbow, so I had to wear my electric blue shirt underneath. If the aim of this uniform was to conceal my feminine curves, it was all that could be desired.

I spent the rest of the day following Sister Fatma, supposedly being oriented but, as her idea of supervision was to do a lot of shouting at the nurses and I already knew how to shout, I cannot say that I learned much from her. I began to sympathise with the French woman, who told me every time I saw her how confused she was.

I also spent an hour of alleged orientation in hospital

procedures in Len Fitch's office. What I actually heard was a long dissertation on the wrongs perpetrated on him by the company and the MOH, and a series of horror stories about the ill-treatment of expatriates in the kingdom. This did not do much to alleviate my gloom. It appeared I had a bleak year ahead.

At half past five, when I was allowed to leave, I escaped with relief. This must have been the longest day of my life. We started work at a quarter to seven in the morning and did ten-hour shifts. We did this for six days and, on the seventh, praise be, we rested.

After several wrong turns in the concrete jungle, I found my flat, fell on the bed in a state of collapse and, once again, slept like the dead.

An hour and a half later I woke, and with a great effort got up to catch the transport to the village for the weekly shopping expedition. Shops in the kingdom opened from nine in the morning until one in the afternoon, shut for siesta and prayers until five, then stayed open until about nine in the evening. They also closed for half an hour each day during mid-morning and mid-evening prayers, and usually did not open on Friday, the holy day.

Waiting just inside the front gate was the mini-bus that had delivered me inside these locked gates (a thousand curses upon it) complete with the lovely Mustafa. There were about a dozen people on board: doctors, nurses, laboratory technicians, physiotherapists and radiographers. A couple were British, the rest Indian or Filipino. All the women except me wore *abeyas*, and I was determined to buy one as soon as I could.

The village was a few miles away, a collection of mud brick huts huddled along a strip of dusty track beside the highway. Were these the 'extensive shopping facilities' promised in the literature?

On one side there were several shops that sold vegetables and meat. Carcasses of sheep and goats hung in the open in the heat. There appeared to be no refrigeration. Some of the shops did not have electricity but were lit by oil lamps. I call them shops, but they were mud brick, square, flat-roofed huts with roller doors or shutters. You stepped in directly off the street. There were no footpaths. Goods were displayed on crude board shelves or on the ground, with the overflow in the dirt street.

Across the way two shops sold groceries, many of them tinned, and had produce and spices in hessian bags open on the floor. A couple of shops sold pots and pans and cheap plastic items. On a later visit, when I bought a length of cloth, the shopkeeper, eschewing such items as scissors, tore it off with his teeth. One shop sold dresses and women's sandals, catering to the style of the Beduin women. But as it was an *abeya* and not a dinner dress I wanted, this is where I headed.

It took me many weeks to discover all these places, as our shopping time was very limited. An hour a week between prayers should be enough to satisfy the soul of any woman, according to the local way of thinking (male). This first night, I asked one of the other females on the bus where I could buy an *abeya*: it was all I had time to do before the call to prayer sounded, the shop-keepers all went off to the mosque to pray, leaving their shops open, and we had to return to the hospital. My *abeya* cost seventy riyals, or thirty dollars Australian and consisted of large quantities of black silk. I put it on and immediately felt better. Could this be my free spirit now rejoicing in a body veil?

8 The great baggage hunt

I decided to concentrate on rectifying my most urgent problems in order of necessity, and getting my luggage topped the list. All attempts to get Roger Pearce to contact the airport baggage department by phone were unsuccessful; the phone was constantly engaged, and he was unable to send the driver to the airport because he could not get the driver to understand what he wanted done. I finally pressured him into sending me out there. It was not possible to go alone, so I enlisted the company of one of the British female staff, Davina, an Irish radiographer. Normally we would not have been able to travel alone in the hospital bus with a man but, as Mustafa was officially employed as a driver, he had a permit, or something like it, which exempted him and which he showed at any roadblocks we encountered.

We arrived at the airport at half past three and were sent to the customs department where I was told I would find my suitcases. But my joy was shortlived when I discovered that the office shut at half past two. I was told to come back the next day they were open, which was Saturday.

Back at the hospital Roger Pearce said he would organise Mustafa to take me again, and I lined up another chaperone, but Mustafa failed to appear at the appointed time. Either Roger told him the wrong thing, confused him, did not tell him at all, or Mustafa just did not want to go. Roger had told me earlier that it was a waste of time my going to the airport, because I was a woman and the customs officials would give me a bad time. He told me how difficult customs people had been with several male company staff. Len Fitch agreed with him, but neither offered another solution, and I would never have got my luggage if I had waited for them to act. I had deduced that Roger was ineffectual, or did not care, or both, and that Len was downright obstructive. If I wanted anything done, I would have to do it myself.

It took me six days to get my suitcases and, when I read the shipping papers that came with them, I discovered that they had got to Medina before I had and could have been collected on my arrival.

Although I was terrified of the prospect of a confrontation with officious Arab men, my experience with customs was amusing, and we were treated with respect. I put into practice my humble, modest female act, and threw myself on their mercy. Basically Arab men have a certain amount of reverence for women, although this does not necessarily apply to the Bedu, some of whom are pretty basic, the less genteel of them regarding their women as less important than their camels and horses. I once heard women described by a Bedu as 'less than a camel, more than a dog'.

I had the company this time of the Irish sister who lived opposite me. Her name was Sheila, and her age was indeterminate, although she was probably between thirty and forty. She had previous experience in Saudi Arabia and knew how to behave in the company of Arab men. We sat quietly with eyes cast down, utterly subject to their male supremacy and wisdom until we were spoken to, at which times we replied with suitable decorum and modesty. The room we had been shown into was attached to the side of a huge customs shed and was airconditioned. It was a very large room and contained seven very large desks, behind which were seven Saudis all in a state of extreme repose, drinking tea and chatting. Three of the desks were ranged on one side of the room facing three on the other side and the seventh, obviously that of the boss-cocky or director, stood in solitary splendour at the far end facing them all.

The airport official who had brought us in handed us over to the man behind the first desk inside the door. He shuffled my papers for a long time and then passed them back to our escort who, with us in tow, went to the next desk, where the same process was repeated. And so we circulated around the room until finally we stood in front of the director's desk. So far no-one had spoken a word to us. The great man looked up at us and smiling kindly said, 'Please sit down and wait', offering us a chair each at his side and asking us if we would like some tea. It seemed to me that some Saudis were far kinder than the foreigners working for them. I understood that women and men could not eat and drink together unless they were married to each other and in the privacy of their own homes but, even if it were permitted, how could a woman drink a cup of tea without lifting her veil? (It might eliminate the need for a tea strainer.) I was to discover, however, that, as in this case, Saudis with standing in the community seemed to be able to make exceptions for foreign women, because some of them regarded us as honorary men. The tea was very strong and sweet, flavoured with a kind of mint and served in a very small glass mug rather like a miniature beer stein. (Oh! Wash your mouth, you evil infidel!)

Meanwhile the escort went off with my papers, and we

sat in demure silence. I don't think anyone spoke very much English, and it would have been unseemly to chat to us. Wondering about the need for this huge room full of desks and all these people to do one man's job, I concluded that it must be another case of jobs for the boys, or in this case, jobs for the Saudis. There were nine men here, including the escort and the inspector waiting in the shed, and I am pretty sure that mine was the only job they would have had all day. Almost all customs activity takes place in Jeddah or Riyadh.

Twenty minutes later the escort returned, and we were off again following him out into the shed where my two suitcases – Oh! happy sight! – were spread on the floor. They were rather the worse for their adventures. One was battered and dirty and missing a handle, and the other was almost completely demolished, with my belongings hanging out of one end in a most abandoned manner. I was prepared for many things to be missing, but when I checked later nothing had gone. There is something to be said for the law that punishes stealing by cutting off a hand.

The inspecting officer hardly gave the contents a glance and then sent us back to the Room of the Desks, where the whole of the previous procedure was repeated with another set of papers. This time, at each desk, the papers were signed and, at the last desk, another set of papers was made, but we were graciously permitted to sit in our chairs throughout the performance while the escort went from desk to desk. Then I had to sign all the papers and, at long last, was given custody of my cases.

Sheila and I dragged and heaved them into the bus and back to my flat, where we struggled up three flights of stairs with them under the interested eye of Mustafa.

I had finally got my luggage after six long days, and I

had learned some very important lessons. One, the company was never going to be any help to me in this place. Two, if I wanted something done I had better do it myself. Three, if I wanted help I had far more chance with the Saudis. Four, I should not be afraid of the Saudis, as the company seemed to be. And five, I had one thing to my advantage that the company officials did not have, which used correctly could be an asset: I was female and, although this is definitely a big disadvantage most of the time, there were times when it could be made to work for you.

9 In bad repair

Having solved my first problem and revelling in the luxury of a bath-towel and a pillow and sheets, I could now move on to improving my living quarters.

Armed with my hard-won knowledge of how to get things done, I approached a member of the MOH staff and said I had items that needed fixing in my flat. Until now I had been telling Roger daily that I did not have a working fridge or stove, and he had told me daily that he was organising it. But I was through with Roger. He could not organise a booze-up in a brewery. I had lost my girlish innocence in the six nights I had spent without bedclothes, a pillow or a towel because he was too ineffectual to send someone to the airport.

I had discovered that the way to get repairs done was to fill out a requisition form and send it to the housing supervisor. This would then be ignored unless they knew who you were and felt like doing it for you. Roger and Len Fitch seemed to be unaware of this procedure: Len had been making verbal requests and Roger had been forgetting all about it.

The director of maintenance was a charming young Saudi. (All directors of departments have to be Saudi, and MOH employees. Mostly they are there for decoration and the real work is done by a qualified person imported from a neighbouring Arab country, or India, or anywhere.) I gave him my requisition form, and set about mastering the tricky part: how to get the workmen to appear to do the repairs.

I have worked in some backwaters, but I have never been expected to practically build my own staff quarters and then equip them, as I had to do now. Apart from the dirt, there were a few little matters that needed rectifying. The fridge did not work but, on closer inspection, I found this was because it was not plugged in. It was an American fridge and the plug was an Asian one. It seems a small enough matter to get an adaptor plug, but here this was not so easy. The maintenance department did not have any and, when I eventually found one in the *souk* at the village, it had to be modified, which meant finding an electrician. Once I would have tackled the job myself, but since a little episode some years ago involving my Do-It-Yourself electrical repairs and a confrontation by torch-light with an irate hospital engineer in the midst of a complete hospital power failure, I was reluctant.

The stove presented another difficulty. It did not work because there was no gas bottle attached to it. This item had disappeared with the previous occupant. There were also two broken windows, the kitchen sink was blocked, the toilets did not flush, and the seats and lids were broken. There was no hope of replacing the toilet seats and lids as they were not available in the kingdom, so I jettisoned the idea of getting them from somewhere and lived without. They were the last toilet seats I saw in the hospital or quarters for the rest of my stay. When I returned home toilet seats seemed such utter luxury that I found it hard to believe that I had once taken them for granted. Originally toilet seats had been supplied by the builders, but they were all broken by the staff and patients and could not be replaced. It occurred to me that in all my years of living in close association with toilet seats I have never broken one, nor known anyone who has. Perhaps it is not something you talk about in polite company, and if people do break them, they do so in the privacy of their own homes and would not admit to it on the rack.

The hot water service was also broken, as were all the airconditioners except the one in my bedroom. The tap from the kitchen sink lay dejectedly on the bench top, and the sink and the hand basin in the bathroom were blocked. What little furniture I found was either damaged beyond repair or came apart in my hand every time I touched it. I found a dressing table in one of the other bedrooms and dragged it into my room. It had four drawers, all of which had to be reassembled each time I opened them.

I was expected to provide all utensils, curtains, shower curtains (not available anywhere in the kingdom that I had access to), toilet brush, brooms, mops, bed linen, towels and pillows. I was not told about this, but a fifty kilo allowance would not have gone far if I'd brought all that.

The flat was about seven years old and in a block of six, which had been built by a Korean company. The building was functional but ugly, constructed of concrete with terrazzo floors. A staircase of terrazzo went up from the front entrance through the centre of the building, and there was a landing on each floor with two flats, one on each side, to a height of three floors. The entrance door to the flat led straight into the huge communal lounge-diningroom. The bathrooms were fitted with bath and shower, bidet and toilet in institutional white and were appallingly dirty. The paint throughout was off white (very off), which emphasised its grubbiness. The one remaining light fitting was in the 1960s mould. There was a general feeling about the place that it had been built recently with old fittings – perhaps the fashion in Korea – and everything was built on a large scale as was done fifty or sixty years ago. The sparse furniture in the large rooms gave it a desolate air.

My bedroom had a wardrobe, without the benefit of handles, the dressing table had drawers that fell apart and the bed had a saggy wire base. The other bedrooms were empty except for one broken bed lying in pieces in a corner.

The next day I received a message from the maintenance director to say that I should be at my flat at one o'clock, to let the repair crew in. I waited for an hour and a half, but no-one came. The next day we repeated the process, and this time the men arrived, but they were an hour late. I think they were testing me to see if I was really serious. When I showed the workmen the faults in the flat, they said they could only do the airconditioners, that I would need plumbers and 'specialists' for other jobs. Then the airconditioner 'specialists' set to work on the one in the sitting-room, removing the remains of a dead pigeon from the bowels of the machine, spraying feathers all around the room and over the floor. No wonder it hadn't worked (it didn't appear to have done the pigeon a lot of good either). The pigeon out, they asked me for sticking plaster, which I supplied, but even this marvel of modern medicine failed to resuscitate the ailing airconditioner. (Sticking plaster seemed to be the mainstay of the maintenance men. No wonder there was never enough for the patients.) So, saying that they would come back tomorrow and take it to the workshop for further surgery, they departed. I had learned enough to know that the two things could not have been done in one visit.

The day after, the plumbers came and unblocked one sink and, after making a terrible mess, promptly walked out, leaving me to clean up the floor. They had not even had the sense to put a bucket under the pipe before they unscrewed it. They said they would return the following morning. I waited an hour for them, but they did not appear. When I contacted the maintenance director, he said they would be there at one o'clock. To my surprise, they turned up and actually managed to fix the toilet.

Spurred on by this achievement, I showed them the tap that needed replacing in the kitchen. Now, the crew consisted of a Saudi, the supervisor, who did nothing, and a tradesman who was a Pakistani. The Saudi looked at the tap and said, 'It cannot be fixed. We will need to order a new one.' But the Pakistani said, 'No, no,' took out a spanner and had the tap on and working in thirty seconds. The oil-rich approach, I guess, is to throw it away. Another approach, if they could not be bothered, or just plain did not want to fix something, was to order another, knowing that it could take years, if it arrived at all. The words that most closely correspond to *manyana* in Arabic are *Bukra Insha'llah*, which translate as 'Tomorrow, God willing' or, 'If God wills it'. It is the second most widely used phrase in Arabia. The most widely used phrase is *Al'humdallah*, which means, 'Praise be to God'. I was soon using both of these phrases with the best of them and as often as the locals. Someone told me that he had asked a Saudi if they had an expression which meant the same as *manyana*, and he said, 'No, tomorrow would be too quick for us.'

10 The mythical beast

After a never-ending six days since my arrival, it was Friday, the day of rest. I slept a solid twelve hours and then set about scrubbing the interiors of the wardrobe and cupboards.

I had discovered an empty downstairs flat inhabited by a family of wild cats who had made their home in a mattress in the middle of the sitting-room. They seemed to exist mainly on pigeons, judging by the corpses scattered around. That was probably how the pigeon remains got into my flat too, though I could not explain the one in the airconditioner. There were many of these strange wild cats living around the compound, all of a mixed ginger, white and black colouring, and with no tails.

I decided to swipe the shower curtains and a bedside cabinet. They were the only items in the flat that were reasonably intact. The shower curtains were a bilious-coloured plastic, but they were large and opaque and I tacked one across the bedroom window and the other around the shower rail over the bath. I did not bother about the other windows, just being careful not to walk about in a state of undress.

I had also bought a plug for the fridge on my second trip to the village market, and I had found an Indian engineer in a workshop in the bowels of the hospital whom I had persuaded to convert it to fit the plug of my fridge. But I hit a snag with the stove; there was no such thing as a spare gas bottle. They were changed when empty by Maintenance, who popped up out of nowhere, like the Tooth Fairy, and exchanged old for new. But like the Tooth Fairy who refuses to part with the small silver coin unless you have a tooth to donate, the Gas Bottle Man would not give me a new gas bottle unless he was given an old one in return. As mine had been stolen, I had to buy a new one at a cost of sixty dollars. The company was supposed to pay for our gas, but I never did get a refund from Roger, who kept telling me to write him a memo about it, which was his way of avoiding action.

It had taken me six days of hard slogging, but now at least I had the basics and at last could make myself my own cup of tea.

I set about repairing the furniture with the aid of a couple of bottles of glue bought in the *souk*. It looked a bit rough and had occasional relapses requiring further first aid, but I kept the glue bottle at the ready for the whole of my stay. At least the fronts of the drawers no longer came off in my hands or fell on my feet every time I opened them.

The next highlight of my day off was a trip to the compound shop. I had learned by trial and error that the shop shut at prayer time for about half an hour. It was only open between eleven in the morning and one in the afternoon, and four in the afternoon until nine at night, and there were three prayer times during that time, so it became a work of art to time it correctly. I was always arriving to find it shut, or I was just inside the door when the call to prayer sounded and I would be put out again. The shop was run by a Saudi on contract and was always full of Filipino nurses, whose only recreations were going to the shop, cooking and eating. The company was supposed to supply all the charge nurses, supervisors, and more senior people, but it had only four of us on site. The rest of the nurses were all working directly for MOH. They had been recruited from all over Asia, India and Pakistan, but most were Filipinos: 388 of them to be exact. As they worked for MOH they did not have access to the company bus trips out, and spent their entire contracts in the compound. Their contracts were for three years and could not be broken. They could resign, but MOH would not send them home, so there was no point. They had six weeks leave at the end of each year. If they wanted to get out they had to wait until their leave was due, when they would be given a paid return ticket and an exit visa. During that year they were virtual prisoners. The Ministry of Health saw nothing strange in this.

On the ten-minute walk to the shop, I had taken to carrying an umbrella, as the heat was so intense, and I began to think that wearing an *abeya* and covering your head and face was a sensible thing when you were out of doors in this climate. Even the men are never without head coverings, the *gutera* being worn at all times, indoors as well as out.

I did not mind wearing the coverups when I was outside for the protection they gave me from the sun, although it was a bit of a drag having to remember to put them on each time I stuck my nose beyond the door of my flat. But wearing them inside, especially if the building was not airconditioned, was awful. My *abeya* hung on a hook just inside the front door, along with my long black head scarf. It was made of fine black silk and was like a wide sleeveless cape with slits to put your

53

hands through. It reached to my ankles, and it covered my body and arms. With my head wrappings on, all that were presented to the public gaze were my face, hands and feet. The only time I went outside my flat without it was when I was in uniform going to and from work. Then all that could be seen of me were my face and hands, as socks had to be worn in the hospital at all times. Perhaps the sight of my little pink toes would inflame a man's passions too. I was told that my hair would. As the person telling me this had never seen my hair, I wondered how she knew.

The local women were heavily veiled over their entire faces and bodies. They put a black scarf over their heads and faces and then their *abeyas*, draping them from the top of their heads which makes them look even less human than when worn, as mine was, from the shoulders. The British men irreverently called them Guinness bottles, for that is the shape they resembled, especially from the rear. I wondered how they managed to see enough to move around, so I put my black scarf over my face to try it. The scarves are made of heavy, open-weave cotton, and it is possible to see through them dimly, rather like looking through a dark fly screen. How they walk around, without falling over, however, amazed me. I was told that the women suffer a lot from eye and vision problems when they get older.

By now I had examined the compound in full on my walks to and from the shop and the hospital. I had learned that taking an aimless stroll was frowned upon. You might be up to no good trying to meet men, or horrors, have an assignation. Anyone loitering without obvious purpose was confronted by a guard, who would rapidly appear on a motor bike. They either had radar, or someone sent a message to security. Probably the latter.

I was told that European females were watched all the time. It would not have been hard. At that time there were only four others beside me: Jolie the French nurse, Sheila, the Irish nurse, Davina, the Irish radiographer – all company staff – and Cathy, an English nurse who worked for MOH.

The compound was enormous. It housed over two thousand people, about the size of a country town in Australia. Not all the inhabitants worked at the hospital. Many were employed in other MOH hospitals and clinics in Medina, such as the eye hospital, the infectious diseases hospital and a place called Minimal Care, which always left me wondering. The staff of these other hospitals were taken to work and back daily in MOH buses. Apart from the four European females, there were six European men: our fearless leader, Roger, the South African; the fearless leader's deputy, Paul, a Welshman; Len, the world's leading male chauvinist and the chief nurse, a Scot; Rene, a French dentist; Shaun, an Irish dentist; and David, a laboratory technician who came from England. Only some of the King Fahid staff were non-Muslim; all the rest were either Arab, Asian or Indian Muslims. This left us, a minority group, referred to as *Nasrani*, Christian (from the word *Nazarene*), whether we were or not.

The compound was extremely dirty. Some of the Arabs had some very unsavoury habits, such as throwing their rubbish, fatty cooking water and slops out of the kitchen windows. When walking in the compound you had to constantly keep a weather eye out for their missiles.

The compound was situated twenty kilometres from the walls of Medina, in an effort, I guess, to keep the contamination from its heathen inhabitants far from the holy city. It was surrounded by a high wall with turrets at each corner. They are very big on walls in Saudi Arabia. I saw all kinds, with every conceivable ornamentation: turrets, parapets, knobs, swirls, flowers, and lights. Sometimes the walls surrounded a house, but often behind them stretched large areas of nothing. The walls were always great, long, high affairs, and would cost as much as a small house at home.

At one corner of the compound wall, on the road that led to the airport, was the entrance gate with its sentries and guard-house. There was a boom barrier across the road leading in, which the sentry would swing up by means of a rope if you were allowed admission. This was also the entrance to the hospital, and the only way in or out for patients and staff.

On the right, just inside the gate, was the hospital mosque, from which the Mezzuin called the faithful to prayer five times a day. Every local community has its mosque, but all mosques are barred to non-believers. Islam and prayer – *salaat* – are the focus of the way of life, and during *salaat* everything stops. There is no activity except that of the most urgent nature, such as surgical operations. Even phone calls are out: the telephonist spreads his prayer mat on the floor beside the switchboard and says his prayers. People who cannot get to a mosque pray in the street, in their offices, on the desert's dusty face. The sight of a group of men facing Mecca and bowing down in homage to Allah became an accepted part of everyday normal life for me. Prayer times are reckoned by the time of sunrise and sunset, as they start at dawn, and change every day. The frequent call to prayer governed our lives, but I soon became accustomed to it.

Just inside the gate on the left was the hospital block,

a six-storeyed, concrete monstrosity. The hospital's front doors were also watched over by two armed guards, and the Saudi national flag floated above the entrance. It is white on a green background, and has a palm tree above two crossed, unsheathed swords and the words of the Muslim creed in Arabic script beneath: 'There is no God but Allah, and Mohommed is His Prophet.' The palm tree is the Arab traditional symbol of life. It supplies the main agricultural crop and is an emblem of vitality and growth. The swords unsheathed symbolise strength rooted in faith, and the willingness to defend Islam and to fight to further it.

The roads through the compound were gravel and cement. The housing started from behind the hospital and marched back, row after row of concrete blocks stretching to infinity, with nothing to relieve their starkness. The only attempt at relief had been to put a row of trees and shrubs around the perimeter of the hospital. I was told they had been commissioned by the local Emir, the Prince of Medina, and that he paid for their maintenance. This consisted of a visit once a day by a water tanker, which came in early in the morning. A Pakistani fellow trotted along behind it, giving them a blast of water from a hose as thick as a thigh. The poor trees, scraggy, sparse pines, were having a grim struggle against the lack of water and the heat, and failed to do much to adorn the place. In between the trees, very untidy and choked with thriving weeds, a few stunted and tattered lantana and oleander bushes fought grimly to stay alive. There was also an occasional vinca or a zinnia, horribly deprived, but still managing to sport an odd purple or orange flower.

In the centre of the compound was a large concreted open area. On one side was the shop which mainly contained imported food, although some items are made under licence in Riyadh and Jeddah. But most of the food catered to the Arab or Asian taste. There was not much concession made to European preferences in food. Tinned fruit and vegetables and dairy products seemed to be about the limit of my diet. There was a section containing fresh fruit and vegetables, all of which were imported. I heard that much of it came from Israel, but that it was sent through Lebanon or Egypt to make it more acceptable. The prices, subsidised by the government, were much the same as in Australia, except for exotic goods such as ice cream, which was twice the price it is here. There was also a fresh meat counter presided over by an enormous Nubian, whose shiny, round face always wore a beaming smile. The meat in the shop was slightly more attractive than that at the village *souk*, but it was still a long way from the standards of hygiene and presentation that I was used to. And the price was horrific. Meat was something I never bought.

Apart from the food, there were some household items that were mostly plastic and ugly and expensive. The locals love plastic and see it as the height of modernity but scorn the lovely glass and pottery imported from surrounding countries, which is ridiculously cheap and with which I equipped my flat.

On the other side of the compound was the so-called recreation centre. This was the mythical beast I had read about in that work of an over-active imagination, the company propaganda sheet on life at KFH. This building possibly had been intended as a place of recreation by the person who designed it, but he was not a Saudi, or he would have known that recreation is not allowed to employees. So the recreation centre that didn't exist was converted into another mosque, an office for the airline Saudia, and a small bank.

The swimming pool, which also featured heavily in the company blurb, did exist, but it had never been filled with water and so was not a great source of entertainment. I suppose a real fitness freak could have jogged up and down in it, but it's just not the same. The reason for its virginal condition was simple. It could not have been communal, so it would have had to have been used by men and women on different days. This could easily have been arranged, but it would have needed a wall around it for women to use it. If my hair would inflame a man's passions, imagine what the sight of me in a bathing suit would do!

During my sojourn at KFH, the hospital director was always promising the company administrator that the wall would be built and the pool used. Eventually, after continual harassment, the wall was built, but when it was discovered that if you went to the top of the surrounding housing blocks (which were all flat topped and housed the washing lines) and leaned over at a perilous angle, you could see the pool, that was it! It was back to the drawing board. If it had not been for the agitations of the company staff, nothing would ever have been done about it. The MOH workers, such as the Filipinos, had no voice whatsoever. No-one was concerned about doing anything for them. They were there to work, not cavort about in swimming pools. And the Arabs, although they have a tremendous love of water and greatly admire fountains and ornamental devices incorporating it, have little desire to immerse themselves in it.

It was eventually announced that the solution was to be a cover over the top of the pool, but when I left, it still had not materialised, and I doubt that it ever would. It is not the Arab way to say no; it is more courteous to agree but defer your actions.

11 Servants of the king

Meanwhile at the hospital I was still supposed to be receiving orientation from Len Fitch. He blustered and swaggered, seeming suspicious and afraid of women, but he was civil, if paternalistic, to me. He seemed to want people to be dependent on him and preferably unhappy, as this gave him the edge. When I first arrived, for example, I told him that I needed to change some money into riyals. His solution was to lend me some, saying that I could give it back to him on payday (almost a month away). It was not until I had been there for a week that I discovered there was a bank in the compound. After several fruitless visits at the wrong time (it was either shut or it was prayer time), I got inside to find that it was a small branch office of The Arab National, staffed by a couple of Saudi gents who told me that Australian dollars did not exist. I still had some Australian cash in my wallet, and when I showed it to them they were amazed. I was the first Australian in the district apparently. When the time came to send my salary home, however, I discovered that the Saudis are remarkably efficient at banking. There was never any problem with converting or sending money.

My orientation (for want of a better word) consisted of following the supervisor of each floor for a day or two. I think this was because Len Fitch did not know what else to do with me. I had not, as I had been told, been sent here to fill a particular post. There were so few company staff that all but one of the charge sisters and almost all of the supervisors' positions were vacant. In the meantime these jobs were being done by Filipino nurses, who were all paid at the same rate, so they were extremely reluctant to take extra responsibility. The authorities had a nasty way of blaming the nurses for anything that went wrong. In the hospital, nurses were on the bottom of the pecking order, possibly because most of them were women.

I had worked my way up and down the hospital, from floor to floor, following the supervisors for a week, and was getting the distinct impression that none, with the exception of Cathy, the Englishwoman, had much idea what was expected of them. The job description I had been given sounded like an advertisement for Wonder Woman. It gave no clue how you might improve standards and give leadership, and there was no-one to give directions or suggestions. The task was daunting: the entire hospital and nursing care were a shambles.

There were six supervisory staff, including me, but only one, the lumpy French sister, Jolie, belonged to the company. I had thought her strange when I first met her, but after a day in her company I amended my diagnosis to down-right loopy. She was what my father would have called 'not quite the full quid'. She had been at the hospital for several weeks and had not the faintest idea what was going on. She went about muttering, in a sort of litany, 'Oh, what a terreebla place this is.' I could not have agreed more, but I still wished she would shut up.

While we are on the subject of strangeness, I should mention the Irish radiographer, Davina, who solemnly told me, not once but often, that a lot of her problems arose from not understanding what was said to her. She insisted that she had been deaf since they made her take her pierced earrings off because they showed under her headscarf.

Three other supervisors, one female and two males, were Europeans who worked for MOH. They had been recruited directly by the MOH in London. This was not usual, as MOH mostly recruit only Arabs and Asians, but after these people returned and made their treatment known, as they threatened to do, I do not think they would recruit many more.

The female supervisor was the Englishwoman, Cathy, who was the only really good nurse there. Her situation was appalling. She had been told a complete fairytale by her recruiter, who knew the reality very well. At least the recruiter who misled me did so in ignorance. Cathy wanted to get out the moment she arrived but discovered that she was a virtual prisoner in the compound for a year. The MOH made no dispensation for the fact that she was European and recruited in England. She was female and would be treated the same as all the other female workers. She had to live under the same conditions as the Filipinos did. The first night she had to sleep on a mattress on the floor of a room with three other nurses. But the Filipinos are very kind and generous and at least she had help and comfort from them. Cathy was not permitted outside the gate, at any time. The MOH could work her in any position they chose and send her anywhere they wanted. Unless they gave her an exit visa, she could not leave. The company was sorry for her but could do nothing to help, except for allowing her to use the phone to ring the British ambassador in Jeddah. But the might of this august personage was of no avail. He could not, in the end, get her contract revoked. She wrote letters to the official head of MOH because he was in Medina, and there was no other way to contact him. It was almost impossible to get someone on the phone locally, as I remembered from the airport episode. The letters were all intercepted and given to the hospital director, who returned them to her. When her husband called from London, the telephonist refused to put him through to her flat, which was the usual practice.

The fate of the two men was not as bad because, as men, they could walk out of the gate and go to the village. If they wished they could have bought a car and driven to Jeddah. But it is strictly forbidden for any woman to drive a car.

One of these fellows was an Englishman called Arthur, the supervisor of the all-male orthopaedic floor. He did a lot of picking and fussing at the nurses but did not seem to be making any headway. The other was Matthew, a British-trained Indian nurse who had psychiatric qualifications but no general hospital experience at all. He had been recruited and sent out to work as a charge sister at the psychiatric hospital, but when he arrived he discovered that the the psychiatric hospital was in Medina, within the walls, and our hero was not a Muslim. And despite his protestations that he was not qualified to work in a general hospital, they dumped him at KFH until his contract was up. It did not seem to matter that he was fulfilling no useful function and doing nothing to earn his salary. He stood around all day, decoration on one of the wards, and no-one cared. He was promised a transfer 'soon', but I doubt if that went further than the promise.

When I first heard that Matthew had been promised a transfer I hotfooted it to Roger's office to stake my claim. On hearing my request, Roger's mouth fell open. Why did I wish to leave? he asked me. I, in turn, registered my amazement. Didn't he know the place was the pits! 'No-one likes it here! Don't you know what is going on around you?' Roger was not in the same boat as we other Servants of the King. Somehow he had managed to get himself housed at a compound a couple of kilometres further along the road, which had been built to house the staff of a luxuriously appointed private hospital and was very different from the austerity of the government-funded KFH. Here our illustrious leader had installed himself in a three-bedroomed villa, with the use of a pool. He had the company car and went home for lunch, so he never had to eat dining-room meals. And he had brought his wife with him. No other company worker was allowed to bring a spouse and this irritated the other married staff. I believe he genuinely did not know how we poor serfs lived. He had never taken the trouble to inspect any of the housing at KFH, and I think he was convinced that it was the same as his. All complaints ran off him like water off a duck's back. He cruised along, waiting out the couple of years to his retirement, making sure not to upset anyone, doing as little as possible because that was the way to succeed. Only people who did things could get into trouble if anything went wrong. If one of the nurses under my charge did something wrong, for example, I could be held responsible, even though I was in bed at the time. It was no wonder no-one wanted to make decisions or have positions of authority. This rule did not necessarily apply to Saudis, it being generally felt that the point in having foreigners there was to have someone to take the blame when things went wrong.

Roger, for all that, promised me many improvements,

as well as a transfer. I did not believe him and, of course, none of it came to much. I concluded that he was either rapidly advancing into an early senility, or had brain damage from too much booze in a previous life. He had the signs and symptoms of both. I was surprised at the number of heavy drinkers and alcoholics who came to Saudi Arabia. Maybe they came in an effort to reform.

During my first week at KFH I wrote several letters to Alpha in Australia requesting – well, demanding would be more accurate – a transfer (In truth, I abused them.) I think my actual terms were along the lines of, 'Get me out of here or else', and my language was not fit to be printed. I doubted the letters could do much to help me, but I felt better for having said my piece. There was no answer and I naturally thought that they had abandoned me to my fate. Much later, I learned that on receiving my irate epistle they had immediately phoned Roger and asked to speak to me. He had replied that I was unavailable and had told them that I had been upset with Medina at first because I had thought I was going to Taif in the mountains, but that now I was quite happy.

I also learned later that a couple of months after this the recruiters had submitted me for a transfer to a post at the government hospital at Mecca, which was also under Omega Health management. This post was as the chief nurse or director of nursing. I was approved by the company for the job and an application on my behalf was sent to the MOH head office in Riyadh, resulting in my appointment. It was a promotion with a large increase in salary and to a much more habitable area. Mecca is only one hour from Jeddah and an hour from the mountain city of Taif.

When told to arrange this transfer for me, Roger, who

had to obtain the hospital director's approval for it, told him that I was too valuable to lose. The director consequently refused to sign my release and my transfer was cancelled. I was not even told about this at the time and when I learned about it I felt powerless.

It was fortunate for Roger that he had, by the time I discovered his perfidy, removed himself from the country, or I would not have been answerable for his physical safety. I lay awake at night planning to inflict atrocities upon his person: boiling in oil was one of them.

The other two supervisors were females, a Filipino and a Korean. The latter was a short woman, chubby and aggressive. I found the Koreans here more assertive than other Asian women I had encountered. This one was downright bossy. She had the strangest voice – loud and high and squeaky – sounding for all the world like a mouse stuck in a milk bottle.

Instead of allocating me a place to work, Len Fitch told me I could work anywhere I chose. I said that I preferred medicine to surgery, and he immediately said he would move Cathy from the medical floor so that I could have it, adding that she was not a company employee and had to work where she was told. I was aghast at his cold-blooded disregard for the feelings of the staff for, whether MOH or company, they were all under his charge. Having spent two days with Cathy, I knew that she was the best he had. She had worked very hard to improve her floor and would hate to be moved from it.

I declined his offer and elected to take the first floor, which he had told me was the area in the biggest mess and most needing help. It consisted of the intensive care unit, the cardiac care unit, the burns unit and two neurosurgery wards, male and female. I felt that as long as I had to spend some time there I might as well do something interesting, and that if I had a challenging job it might compensate for the lack of stimulus and my lack of freedom.

The first floor had eighty-five beds: fifty in the neuro-surgery wards, fifteen in intensive care, five in cardiac care and fifteen in the burns unit, although this ward was actually elastic and I saw up to twenty-five patients crammed into it in the burns season. Sometimes a whole family would be admitted at the one time. The Bedu and the villagers use kerosene and methylated spirits for cooking and for fires during cold nights in the desert. There were many accidents and young children died frequently as a result of burns.

The nurses on the first floor were, as in the rest of the hospital, a mixture of Arab, Asian and Indian, although most were Filipinos. The floor was badly organised, the nursing care poor and the place dirty, cluttered and untidy. My job would be tough.

When I fully understood the situation at the hospital, it was clear that the difficulties were that the company did not have sole management of the place, but were joint managers with MOH, and that the company did not have enough staff at the site to make any impact. They were only contracted to fill about sixty senior management positions, and as yet had only twenty-two staff, ten Indians and Arabs and twelve Europeans. In a five hundred-bed hospital, with a total staff of around a thousand, this meant that managers were hopelessly outnumbered.

It was a task rather like trying to push water uphill, requiring a huge effort that many people, like Roger, were not prepared to make. I chose to fight to improve my floor because I would not have been able to tolerate the boredom of doing nothing, and I have always enjoyed a challenge and a bit of mortal combat.

The MOH obstructed the company at every opportunity and criticised the company staff continually, sometimes unfairly, but often with just cause. But they did not understand that there were not enough of us to make a noticeable improvement in a short time.

Most of the administration staff were Saudi, who either had no qualifications whatsoever, or qualifications of dubious validity. The rest were Egyptian, or from other surrounding Muslim countries, such as Ethiopia and The Sudan, as were the doctors, with the exception of several Indians who had qualified in Britain. The ancillary staff were the same. Of the total five hundred and sixty nurses, three hundred and eighty-eight were Filipino, about ten of whom were men. There were one hundred and thirty-seven female Koreans, eighteen female Indians, seven female Egyptians and a few Jordanians, Palestinians, Somalians and Ethiopians, some of whom were male.

The company's ancillary staff were mostly Sudanese, Ethiopians and Indians who had British qualifications but could be obtained more cheaply than British staff.

The contract the company had with MOH was to supply the management staff for the hospital: the chief administrator, key clerical posts, chief engineer, chief pharmacist, the chief and several other radiographers, stores manager, chief medical officer and several medical heads of departments, as well as the hospital matron (chief nurse or director of nursing), and all charge nurses and nursing supervisors. All other positions were filled by MOH, as were the company posts until company staff arrived.

Among the nursing staff there was an overall lack of interest in the work and care of the patients, which I found strange and disheartening. I discovered that headhunters, the irreverent term used for recruiters, were not in the least concerned with the ability or suitability of the person they sent to do a particular job. They were only interested in the amount of commission they collected for your scalp. And once they had you *in situ*, and they had the thirty pieces of silver for your body, as far as they were concerned their job was finished and you were on your own.

Eventually I came to see that the reason I was not as desperately unhappy as most of the others was that there is far more dissatisfaction among people who are forced to work under stressful conditions than those who choose it in a spirit of adventure.

The real head of the hospital was the hospital director, a Saudi with no qualifications or experience. This was, I found, no obstacle to obtaining a position for a Saudi. Your friends and relatives were important credentials. The director was gigantic and fearsome, looking as though he had just galloped in from the desert on his camel after a wild raiding and killing spree. His name was Jamil, which means beautiful in Arabic, but which was in his case a frightful misnomer, for a more plain-looking villain would have been hard to find.

The obstructions started at the top and were found on all levels. By decree all departments must have a Saudi head, or director, as well as a company one. The Arab distrust of foreigners was almost pathological, bordering on paranoia. This led to some awful situations. A highly qualified and experienced Scottish radiographer arrived, for example, to take up the position of the chief radiographer, but he found that there was already a chief in this department, the Saudi director of radiography. The latter was an X-ray technician, trained in Egypt, whose standards and qualifications were highly suspect. The X-ray department was in chaos. When the company radiographer tried to take charge, the Saudi director of radiography refused to acknowledge him and tried to set him to work as a junior technician. Confrontation ensued, and for three months the poor company chap sat either in his quarters or in the hospital (the Saudi would not let him in the X-ray department), doing nothing and waiting for the hospital director to settle the matter. In the end the Saudi won, and the company person was sent back to the UK.

In other cases the Saudi head of department would allow the company head to work alongside him. This meant that the company person did all the work, took all the responsibility, usually having to make do with a broom closet to work in while the Saudi lounged in his opulent office entertaining his friends and drinking tea.

It was not too long or arduous a day for the Saudis either, as the government set different hours for them from the heathen help. While company staff worked the minimum of a fifty-hour, six-day week, and were expected to work extra, without the benefit of overtime pay, any time they were ordered (considerably extra for nurses), the non-Saudi MOH only worked forty hours over six days, with no meal break times deducted and with time off to pray if they were Muslim. But the Saudis worked only five days. And I use the term loosely. These lucky people arrived at work supposedly at seven o'clock but actually trickled in from half past seven. They would immediately fall upon the task at hand, which was to stroll up and down the corridors kissing all their mates firmly on both cheeks and set about the serious business of drinking tea. This consumed their time until the first call to prayer at about eleven, when they would saunter off to the mosque for about half an hour. On their return they needed to refresh themselves with more tea to sustain themselves until lunchtime at one.

No-one expected a Saudi to work after half past two, as this was the time for all right-minded persons to lie down for their siestas, until it was time for the late afternoon prayer. They 'worked' these none too burdensome days from Saturday to Wednesday and had Thursday and the holy day of Friday as days off in which to restore themselves for the next week's hard grind.

Meanwhile the company slaves started work at a quarter to seven and worked until half past five or six, with either half hour or an hour for lunch, if you were lucky enough to get away.

12 Lost in a lift

After much soul searching, I decided to stay until my first leave at about three months. I had learned that the way to get out of the country with the minimum of fuss was to go on leave and not return. It was much easier than trying to resign and get an exit visa from a disgruntled government.

I opted to work on the first floor knowing it was supposed to be difficult to manage. So, at the beginning of my second week, I fronted my floor, curiously dressed in my outsize jacket and pants and white, long-sleeved singlet visible from the elbows down, a sight that would have amazed people at home where it is not usual, at least not in the circles in which I move, to wear your underclothes on the outside of your gear. A long white rectangular head scarf wound round my head and neck and my white duty lace up shoes finished off my ensemble. Keeping the nurses dressed in a manner guaranteed not to arouse the interest of the male patients seemed to be a major preoccupation of the hospital director, who issued frequent bulletins threatening punishment for misdemeanours of dress, including wearing jewellery, the showing of the feminine form, or 'polishing' of the lips.

On closer inspection the first floor was the same as the rest of the hospital – overcrowded and dirty –

although well built and modern in design. Much that had been part of the original plan and equipment had been broken and not replaced. Once the builders were gone that was it, and what wore out was gone forever. The builders did not care, and the Saudis, in their innocence, did not realise that it would happen. This had been going on all over the country. When the hospital was being equipped, they had been sold pumps and other items that would need regular maintenance by technicans who were not available in the country. Other fittings and equipment supplied were obsolete or superseded stock that had been off-loaded on the unsuspecting Saudis at top prices. Some goods, like the housing furniture, were inferior in quality, but had been supplied as first class and priced accordingly. Others were exceptionally high quality and expensive, because the Saudis, not caring about expense, always ordered the best, and some firms did the right thing and actually sent it.

The lack of functioning equipment and essential supplies did not seem to worry the hospital director or the MOH management staff. We were expected to get along as best we could with what we had. But the continual shortage of necessary supplies was frustrating to cope with daily. There were never enough dressings, bandages or drugs to go around.

The nurses, by my standards, were slow and shoddy, showing little concern for the patient, victims of poor training. Their superior, whom I replaced, was a Filipino well past the first flush of youth who strongly resembled a discontented toad. Resenting her demotion she went out of her way to avoid or misdirect me.

The doctors, with the exception of two British-educated Indians who were company staff, were MOH and some were poorly educated. They had been recruited from Egypt, India, Pakistan and other Arab countries. The best doctors were the Sudanese who had been trained in the UK and whom I found to be kind, gentle and intelligent. But my favourite was an Ethiopian who helped me in my struggles to improve my floor. I encountered only a few Saudi doctors and they were both good and bad. Some had been trained in the UK in prestigious establishments and were excellent: some had qualified in Egypt and were alarming. A surgeon at our hospital once did an appendicectomy and, without noticing it, put a cut in the bowel. Two days later he was most surprised when the patient developed peritonitis and promptly died. The Saudi doctors, for all that, were, after the Sudanese, the gentlest and kindest to the nurses and were well liked among the staff. A couple of them were also excellent practitioners.

The worst doctors I encountered were the Egyptians. Corruption is such in Egypt that it is possible to pass exams and gain a degree by bribery or by paying someone else to sit the exam for you. Some of the Egyptian doctors I saw in action certainly suggested that this is how they were qualified. Some of them, however hopeless as medicos, were disastrously good-looking and utterly charming.

Often the Egyptian doctors treated the Filipino nurses arrogantly, like servants or slaves, which made them unpopular. They were also lazy, and made the already over-worked nurses do as much of their work as they could. Some of them even brought their personal washing to the nurses and ordered them to do it. And the nurses did so. As Egypt is Saudi's closest Muslim neighbour, with low wages and high employment, MOH recruited most of its doctors there.

The Arabs in general treated Asians rather badly. They felt them to be inferior, as did the Indians. The Saudis had no colour prejudices but were snobs about genealogy. Their lineage being so pure, they could afford to be, for they have had no influxes of immigrants or conquerors to dilute their aristocratic blood: the Bedu say they can trace their ancestors directly back to Abraham.

The patients, thank goodness, were unaware of anything amiss, as it was only in the last seven years that there had been a hospital, or any medical attention at all in their district. When they did complain it was because the nurse had stepped on their prayer mat or taken away their boiled sheep (smuggled in for them by their loving relatives when they heard that they had been placed on a diet).

Everyone, nurses and doctors alike, lived in mortal dread of the patient who, with the slightest provocation, could report them to the hospital director. No matter how silly or baseless the complaint, it was never ignored. I tried to imagine the situation where any patient, at any time, could wander into the office of the director of the Royal Adelaide Hospital, where I trained and, without knocking, walk through his door, sit in a chair and complain that the nurse forgot to put the orange juice on the tray at breakfast. He would not have got very far. It did happen in Saudi Arabia. A full investigation ensued and the offending nurse was punished.

It is Arab custom that hospitality is hallowed and that all men are equal under God and should at any time be able to come before their leader and seek his counsel. This is why the hospital director's office door was open at all times to all comers. The local prince is available every day in his palace to discuss complaints and grievances, as is the king himself. Any man – wandering Bedu, truck driver or business man – can appear at the palace at audience times to speak with the king and share his coffee and dates. The king is a highly visible leader and member of the faithful, and the success of the House of Saud as rulers is due to the accessibility of those in power. The king is first and foremost the Emir – a local ruler of either a village or a tribe, the enforcer of Islamic ways. Abdul Aziz Ibn Rahman al Saud, the first king of Saudi Arabia who gave the country its name – literally, Arabia of the Sauds – assumed the title of Imam, or law giver, making himself also the defender of the faith and the religious leader. Later he took the further title of Sheik of Sheiks, or king.

As a nursing supervisor I was also rostered as hospital nursing administration sister for afternoon and night shifts (even though my contract did not include night duty), as many as three days a week. This meant that continuity of any programme implemented could not be maintained, because as soon as the supervisor left the floor, the nurses would revert to their old practices. During the day the deputy and assistant chief nurses filled the administration sister's post between them.

I did a couple of evening shifts with one of the other supervisors, and then I was on my own. The evening and night supervisor's job involved doing rounds of the entire hospital, checking all the wards and departments, seeing that all charge nurses were managing their wards satisfactorily, and coping with any problems that arose, such as emergency operations, staff illnesses and replacements, major accidents, cardiac arrests, transfers of patients to other hospitals, complaints from patients, relatives, doctors and nurses and any other human dramas.

The hospital was rarely quiet. Casualty went flat out twenty-four hours a day. There were horrific road accidents. The Saudis drove like maniacs, and no-one wore seat belts. Emergency operations were frequent, and there were never enough beds for all the patients requiring admission.

My share of the evening shifts amounted to about two a week, and night duty comprised one six-night stretch every month. Walking on the upper floors at night, along the wide, empty corridors in that alien place, I felt an eerie sense of detachment.

After working the night duty roster of six nine-hour nights, we were only given one day off, which was in effect only a sleeping day, and then we went back on day duty. This left you exhausted.

It took me a while to familiarise myself with the hospital, because it was very big and had all sorts of nooks and crannies. Arabic was spoken universally and was the only language written on anything, so that, for example, when I got into the lift I did not know where to get out, because the floor buttons had Arabic numbers on them. I was constantly lost, and the security guards stationed on each floor got used to turning me around and sending me off in the right direction.

The hospital had six floors and a basement. All floors had a hundred beds divided into four wards, except the first floor, which had the speciality wards with fewer beds. Male wards were on one side of the floor and female the other, strictly segregated by big dividing doors presided over by security guards. The male patients wore a hospital robe that was very similar to the regular long white *thobes* they wore every day. The women wore hospital nighties, which were huge, tent-like apparatuses. As soon as they ventured out of bed, they donned their *abeyas*. Most of them still wore their scarves, even in bed. Very few ever uncovered their hair, and some retained their face veils. When a doctor was coming a warning was given and everyone promptly dropped their scarves or veils over their faces. I have seen a woman in labour with her nether regions exposed to all in the delivery room, but her face and hair all chastely and primly covered. The doctor was the only male who was given access to female wards, and he had to be at all times chaperoned by a female nurse. Male nurses could only work in male wards, although females could work in both. A woman being seen in outpatients or clinics would be accompanied by her husband or father, possibly several female relatives and a nurse for good measure.

The top floor, the sixth, housed the medical and ear, nose and throat wards. The fourth floor had chest and heart. The third was all male and all orthopaedic, which is self-explanatory, in that women are not allowed to drive and do not go out much. (Almost all cases on this floor were the result of motor vehicle accidents.) The second floor was surgical, and the first I have already described.

The ground floor housed the X-ray department, the pharmacy, the laboratory, the nursing administration offices, the secretaries' offices, the medical superintendent's office, and the library. The basement was where most of the Saudi staff spent their days in the administration offices. Here also were the stores department, the lecture room, the company administration office and the physiotherapy department, complete with a heated swimming pool that no-one was allowed to use.

Tucked away in the darkest corner of the basement, without any windows and in a very confined space, was the prisoners' ward, where inmates were sent for treatment. All prisoner patients were chained hand and foot like animals. They had manacle irons and chains on their wrists and shackles on their ankles; some were also chained to their beds. In the corridors upstairs I passed them shuffling and clanking along, being taken to X-ray or other departments. I found this distressing, as I did the dismal conditions in which they were kept behind a locked wall of bars and wire netting. Attached to this airless hole was a small office where one male Arab nurse and two gaolers kept watch over them. The entire place was as dirty and uncared for as the prisoners were. The Saudis believe that you have been sent to prison because you have offended God primarily, as the country's laws are all based on the rules of the Koran, and secondly society, and that prison is a punishment and not to be made at all pleasant. Rehabilitation is not considered, only retribution. I believe that our hospital ward was like the Hilton compared to life in prison. At least in the hospital the prisoners were fed. In the prison no meals are provided. The prisoner's family or friends had to bring food for him. I wondered what would happen to a prisoner who was a stranger in the country and had no family or friends. I gathered that it would be possible to pay a warder to bring food, providing you had money. In city prisons, one large cell for short-term use can contain five hundred men with not enough room to sit or lie down and only one toilet. Being involved in a traffic accident can result in time spent in a prison cell such as this. In smaller places the conditions and treatment are usually worse. Almost all prison sentences include a whipping, and it is usually from fifty lashes upwards. But that is not the end of it, for the sentence of a whipping is a continuing one, and every Friday, after the main prayers of the day, the hapless offender is taken out to the front of the mosque, which is the traditional place of punishment, and given a further whipping, just to keep his mind on the job of repentance. There cannot be a great many sentenced prisoners in the gaols or it would take all their time to get through it. I believe that the severity of the retribution imposed for crimes in the kingdom does act as a severe deterrent to possible ill-doers.

On the day on which I officially took charge of my floor, the first thing I did was to put a large no smoking sign in the nurses' office of each ward. This small room off the nurses station was supposedly for the charge nurse to work in, but it had been commandeered by the doctors who used it to lounge about and hide in, smoking and idling. The doctors did not do rounds and then disappear as they do at home, only reappearing on the wards when needed, but had to be present on the wards at all times during their rostered duty hours. Consequently, as there were far too many of them in ratio to the patients (in contrast to the extreme shortage of nurses), they spent a lot of their time doing nothing. They also took a lot of time going to and from the mosque to pray, as well as to meals in the dining-room, which accounted for a great deal of the day. The Egyptian doctors also excelled at finding places to sleep.

I had decided that my first concern should be to get the place clean and the nurses working efficiently and to do this I had to get the doctors out from under their feet. As almost all the doctors smoked heavily, when they found that they could no longer smoke on the wards, they began to look for alternative places to pass their time.

I had a lot of trouble convincing the nursing staff that

it was essential to get their wards clean. But with a great deal of persistence I managed to improve the cleanliness of the wards so that I could move on to upgrading the standard of patient care.

On the Thursday of my second week I received my first letter. It was from the customs department at the airport, informing me that my baggage was waiting to be collected; it had been written two days after I had picked it up. The post office is Saudi run, and many letters that I sent home by regular air mail never arrived. There was no point sending registered mail either, as it was not possible to seal registered letters or parcels, because they had to be open for inspection and censorship. Arriving parcels would be opened by customs and sent on, either with the contents half missing, or hanging out in disarray; they were not re-sealed. For Christmas one of the British men received a padded post bag as a present from his mother: possibly that was not the intention of his loving relative, but that is what he got.

Mail was censored and infringements of the law were heavily penalised. We were advised to inform all our relatives and friends to be most careful of what they wrote, as any controversial topic could bring the recipient of the letter much trouble. When writing letters home we were told not to include any adverse comments about the country, people, religion or working conditions, as any critical remarks could bring a penalty down upon us. Nothing that could be seen as unfavourable to Muslim beliefs or practices is allowed, nothing offending the *Wahibbi* moral standard, and no political commentary on the House of Saud. Even letters carried by hand were subject to inspection and censorship at customs. Mail to countries that did not have diplomatic ties with Saudi Arabia, such as Israel, was forbidden and would not be accepted by the post office.

The same censorship applied to magazines and books; the *Matawain* – The Committee for the Prevention of Vice and the Protection of Virtue – the religious police, kept a legion of workers employed with ink and brush blotting out anything they did not destroy. *Time* magazine would be offered for sale with half its pages removed, and the remaining ones heavily smeared with black ink covering arms, legs, shoulders, or advertisements for alcohol or cigarettes.

13 A little airing

During the week a notice appeared on the board in the company office stating that there would be a Friday trip to Yanbu, a town on the Red Sea two hundred kilometres to the west, and slightly north, of Medina. By now, after ten days of being locked in the compound, with only two short trips to the *souk*, I was desperate to get out. I promptly put my name on the list for a permit.

The day of rest dawned and, clutching my permit duly signed by the hospital director, I presented myself at the front gate. There, just inside the entrance, Laughing Boy, alias Mustafa the Sour, awaited with the mini-bus. There were eight of us aboard, and we collected another twelve people two kilometres along the road where Omega had the management of another hospital. This filled the little bus almost to bursting. There were nine Europeans at this hospital and they, and those at KFH, made up the entire European community of the Medina district.

The trip took three hours each way. The mini-bus had been designed as shuttle transport for short trips and also for the Japanese who, judging by the space allotted for legs, must have shorter limbs than we do.

A few kilometres from Medina we encountered the checkpoint where all traffic has to stop and an examination is made of everyone's papers. No-one leaves a district without these. At first the scenery along the way was uninspiring, a succession of stones and dust, very dry and with not a speck of green. Everything was the same in shades of grey and beige, but it was so bright that it hurt your eyes to look at it without sunglasses. After an hour we began to climb higher, and the road started to wind through a range of mountains, not very high and consisting almost entirely of bare rock. They looked extremely old – their tops flattened, and on them huge reefs of weathered rock had been exposed by centuries of wear – and I wondered whether they contained a wealth of precious gems.

Now the countryside was made up of low dunes, broken land covered with gravel, the odd bit of grey wiry scrub and stretches of sand. By the side of the road were occasional flocks of goats, and once we passed a small herd of camels. It was amazing that they found anything to eat. Twice we passed an oasis, a miracle in this dry country, formed where subterranean water is close enough to the surface to bubble forth in a spring, or where a well has been dug and camel-driven pumps bring up water to irrigate the surrounding soil. The oases were fenced in and were obviously very valuable.

We drove through several small towns and villages, with the usual square, flat topped, beige or cream-coloured houses, and dusty, stony streets and lanes reflecting the glare. Only one village was different, an ancient settlement of mud brick and stone buildings, some of them crumbling, called Al Hamra. Parts of it were still inhabited, and a new village had been built close by. It was one of those villages in northern Arabia that are so old that some of their names are recorded in the book of Genesis.

We stopped twice on the way, once for Mustafa to

pray, which he did by the side of the road on sand that looked as fine as flour (while we sat in the bus and fried as he had turned off the airconditioner), and another when he decided to have his lunch at a road-side petrol station. The cafe was a primitive affair, being merely a flat roof supported by several pillars, open on all sides to the air. It sat in the middle of nowhere in desolate, desert country, but must have been a place where a few locals and nomads came at night, for there were couches for reclining on, funny, rough wooden structures that appeared to have been hastily knocked up out of discarded four-by-four fencing posts. To one side of them stood a veritable regiment of *hookahs* (the smoking type and not the ladies of the night kind), waiting for the night-time rush hour. To one side was a primitive mosque, no more than a roof with four pillars, like the cafe in miniature. The kitchen was a lean-to on one side, separated from the cafe by a couple of waist-high fridge boxes, half a wall and some chicken wire.

It was another hour before we arrived at the outskirts of Yanbu. Here we came to the first stop light I had seen in the kingdom. It was supervised by a traffic policeman. No-one would have stopped otherwise.

The climate of Yanbu is no milder than Medina for all its proximity to the sea. It is also subjected to the dreaded sand storm, being open to the winds off the sea that can whip the beach sand into a frenzy, as well as the winds coming off the desert from the other direction. On a later trip there, while coming towards the town on an open stretch of road, we were caught in one such storm. Visibility became almost nil and it was like being in a thick, beige fog. The sand beat on the bus with a horrible noise while the *shimoon*, the nasty, hot desert wind, howled around us. There was nothing to do but stop and wait for the hour or so it took for it to pass.

On the outskirts of the town we took a turn which led, after about twenty minutes, to the beach, where we planned to swim. It felt very biblical, and at last I could say that I had bathed in the legendary Red Sea.

The humidity was high in contrast to Medina's dryness, and it was hot and unpleasant walking about in my *abeya*. There were no other women in the streets, and I felt uncomfortable because all the men stared, although no-one spoke to us or bothered us in any way. I did not mind that Mustafa had restricted our shopping time by telling us, in pantomime, that he would leave at seven o'clock. I was waiting for him at that time: I did not trust him not to leave without anyone who was late. We heathens were the least of his worries.

It was almost sundown by the time we set off on the long ride home, and as soon as we had cleared the town Mustafa stopped the bus to say his prayers. Walking a little way off into the desert, he spread his mat, turned to Mecca, stood, then knelt touching his forehead to the ground. Against the setting sun in this empty place, his silhouette had a mystic aura.

14 Alone at last

I had continued to nag Roger about the flat I had been promised. Now he told me that something had been arranged, so I went to look at it. It was what they called a bachelor flat: a bed sitter, quite large, with separate bathroom and kitchen. Previously these flats had been given only to senior male staff members or, in the case of ones like this in the female area of the compound, they had been lived in by two or three single women. It was unheard of for a female to live alone, and the Arabs, Filipinos and Indians did not want to, it was a foreign concept to them. That does not mean that they liked the way MOH crammed them into flats. They would have liked their own rooms, especially as they all worked different shifts. Once I went to visit a nurse who was sick, and there were four beds in her room. This left only just enough room to sidle past between them. There was one nurse who was on night duty trying to sleep and two more who were on their days off. There were sixteen women living in that flat, which was the same as the one I was inhabiting.

All housing was under the control of MOH, so the next morning I had to front to the housing building to sign for possession of the new flat. After being sent in and out of many offices and having explained my mission to various Saudis, I was finally seated in front of a desk in the presence of the one whom I took to be in charge. Believe it or not, there was a camp bed alongside this desk on which a male body was sleeping under a blanket.

To my surprise and embarrassment, the housing supervisor facing me across the desk was the Saudi who had appeared with a set of keys to let me into my bedroom on my first morning. He certainly remembered me. As I was leaving he said to me, 'I shall come to visit you and talk to you about your country.' It was not what I had in mind. The penalty for adultery was death by beheading for him and by stoning for me. Being alone in a room behind a closed door with a man who is not a first blood relative or one's husband may be classed as adultery, which is why office doors always stood open in the hospital. If it was absolutely essential for a man to have a private interview with a woman, the door could be shut only if there were two or more other females present, preferably Saudi, or at least Muslim.

It was only after I had signed a mountain of paperwork that I realised I had admitted responsibility for all the furnishings, and the condition of the interior of the building. If anything was missing when it was time for me to leave, I would have to pay for it, or I could be held without an exit visa until I did. The exit visa was not granted until a form was signed by all the heads of departments in the hospital to the effect that they had no claim on the person requesting the visa. As I did not know what I had signed for, or what was supposedly in the flat, I was at their mercy and could be in for a lot of trouble.

With that obstacle overcome, all I had to do was get the place cleaned and move in. Roger told me that housing would organise cleaning, but I eventually gave up on that idea and cleaned it myself, working in the evenings after I finished at the hospital. It would be impossible to describe the state of that flat. Suffice to say that I started with a broom and followed with a hose down, and that was just the fridge!

By the end of the week I had completed enough of the basics to move in, and I later finished the job gradually when I was off duty.

On the next day of rest, I made the move. The director of stores had said that I could take some of the furniture, such as it was, from the old flat as there was none in the new one except a couch and some built-in cupboards, and that he would ask Roger to organise it. No hope of that, I thought. Roger couldn't organise an orgy in a house of ill repute. I went off to fix it myself.

I asked my friend the Saudi cleaning supervisor how I could do it, and he said I should ask the director of housing. I tried phoning, but no-one answering the phone spoke any English, and I got the usual treatment, so I went over there and elicited a promise that many cleaners would be sent to help me move.

In the end neither Roger's movers nor the housing department's showed up, so I went to my floor and offered two of the male cleaners some money to help me. They did not want any money, but I paid them anyway. The cleaners all belonged to a Lebanese company that had a contract with the MOH to provide the cleaning services for the hospital and compound. Most of these cleaners were male Pakistanis who had been lured there with the promise of good wages, much higher than they would receive at home, where it was difficult to find a job at any price. Some of them were educated and cultured men.

They were worked twelve hours a day, seven days a

week and were rarely, if ever, paid. Their shifts were from six in the morning to six at night, vice versa on the night shift. They had no meal breaks. Their company made mine, villain though it was, look like Little Lord Fauntleroy. When I arrived they had not been paid for seven months and during the following year they were only paid twice. They were not given free food and were housed by their company in the villages around the hospital, where I believe the conditions were unspeakable. What could they do? Strikes and unions are illegal in Saudi Arabia. They could not go home as they had no money and their employer would not get them an exit visa until their contract was completed. Their initial contracts had said that they would be paid six hundred riyals a month, but since they had arrived the company had cut that amount to three hundred. I did not think that their company ever intended to pay them. Most of the cleaners were men who had families depending on them to send money home. Picking a company was rather like buying a lottery ticket, for although many of the companies were bad, some were bona fide. Unfortunately, there was no way of finding out, except by trial and error. At one stage the workers organised a meeting with the company who offered them forty dollars – for full settlement of the seven months owing to them.

Eventually some of them got fed up and went out and camped in the desert, living in communes and supporting themselves.

At the hospital they lived off the charity of others, obtaining food from the staff, or from any of their friends who could purloin it from the kitchen. I know there was a great deal of kindness and charity shown to them by some of the Saudis and their other brother

Muslims. Even the much maligned Christians helped them when they could. Most of us felt terribly sorry for them.

Once I realised the cleaners' predicament I made sure that the ones on my floor were fed. I did this by ordering several extra meals each day for phantom patients, and I told the cleaners that they could eat these in the pantry with the door shut. It was a misdemeanour for anyone to be caught eating or drinking on duty, not because they were eating the patients' scraps, but because they were eating when they should have been working. From the beginning I let it be known unofficially that I turned a blind eye to anything that the nursing staff or others might do to feed the cleaners.

To move me to the new flat, the cleaners made at least six trips carrying the furniture and my baggage. With the aid of a shopping trolley I had borrowed from the shop, I moved the rest of my belongings on my own in the blistering sun. I collapsed in a heap on the bed shortly after sundown, slept until morning, and spent the next three weeks in my off-duty time unpacking and cleaning until I had a reasonable place in which to live. Then I embarked on a repeat of the Repair Performance that I had successfully completed in the other flat, until everything I needed was in working order.

The interior of my new flat, apart from the dirt, was much better than the old one. The living, sleeping, dining area was very large and had room for a table under the window as well as the bedroom furniture and the couch. There were two windows, but they were never opened, because it was necessary to have the airconditioner on at all times. One window looked towards the gate and the mosque just by it, and the other looked across the back of the compound. Far in the distance I could see hills that formed the outskirts of the town of Medina; a big improvement on the prison-like wall that blocked the view from my other flat. At night I could see the lights of the city on and around those hills. It was a strange feeling to be able to see proof of a place that I could never visit except on pain of death.

My flat also had a good-sized kitchen and bathroom. It was fitted – scarcely the correct word – throughout with a good-quality light brown carpet, which looked as though it had been laid by a chimpanzee with a knife and fork; all creases and bumps. The bathroom had, to my delight, a washing machine. It was the front-loading sort, with a little window through which you could spy on your clothes while they were getting clean. In almost a month it was the first washing machine I had seen. I had previously done my washing in the bath.

Finally I had persuaded Roger to find a tailor to make some uniforms – pants and jackets – for me. This entailed getting someone to come out from Medina and, after many false starts, a tailor finally arrived. I went down to the Omega office to be measured, taking with me the Palestinian assistant chief nurse as chaperone. The tailor, a portly Saudi, had brought his assistant to protect him and Roger had his deputy and the male secretary present. The door was, of course, left open as an added precaution. The Company Male Contingent made a few jokes about the fact that the measurer came back for a second attempt to measure my chest and waist, but the tailor and his assistant did not speak English. I afterwards wondered how much Arabic the assistant could understand because, when the uniforms arrived, three complete sets of them, they were the most amazing shape. They were enormous in the legs and seat, but I could not get the front to meet anywhere from the waist up. Obviously they would not do. They were sent back, and the tailor came again to measure me. He seemed a bit aggrieved, as though I had deliberately changed my shape in the last two weeks. That was the last we ever saw of him, and no more uniforms turned up. I found this understandable when I discovered that Roger, in his wisdom, had paid him in advance. Another tailor was found who lived in the village outside the walls. He and the essential assistant arrived and measured me. When this lot of uniforms came, another three sets, they were not much better: this time each was a different shape and size. None was wearable. It was plainly impossible to wear something with a three-inch gap across my chest, or which failed to pass around my middle. A message was sent to the tailor to present himself again, but that gentleman, obviously scenting trouble, prudently failed to reappear and was never seen again. And, yes, Roger had paid him before I tried the uniforms on.

A little later the Saudi who ran the compound shop brought a tailor and his assistant from the Philippines and opened a small tailoring business in a room in the front of the shop. His aim was to cater for the Arab male population trade by making their *thobes*. Most men who could afford it had their *thobes* made to order. There was a sign on the door of the tailor's room that said, 'No Females Allowed', but I got around this by sending a message to the tailor asking him to come to the Omega office, where once again I was measured. In a short time the Filipino tailor produced for me three perfect uniforms, all-covering and shapeless, at a fraction of the price the others had charged. He also altered the parts of the other sets that were salvageable and made three more to fit me. It had taken sixteen weeks to get a full set of uniforms.

At work after my fun-filled day off, there were two interesting happenings. The first was a letter from someone at home, for which I had longed. I had tried a few times to phone my family, but I had not been successful. There were two public phone boxes at the entrance gates, next to the guardhouse, but apart from the fact that they were mostly not working (at one time they were both out of order for an entire month), they were always in demand by a long line of nurses phoning the Philippines. As Australia was seven hours ahead of Saudi Arabia, timing a phone call was a work of art. It was always very noisy at the gate, and at times it was impossible to hear for the traffic coming in and out. It was also close to the mosque, so that when prayer time came the noise of the *mezzuin* calling from the minaret made it difficult to hear. If that did not deter you, the sentry would come over and, without a word of warning, put up his hand, pull down the receiver cradle, and cut you off. No phone calls are permitted during prayers.

I once made a special phone call home for my brother's birthday and, as that day fell on a Friday when I was visiting Jeddah, I made the call from the hotel. It cost me sixty Australian dollars for three minutes and a near heart attack. At one time the telephone was not working properly, allowing you to make free calls, and the sentry arrested an Egyptian nurse he saw using it and called the police. She was charged with theft and deported.

I had gone to the bank during my second week to buy some coins for the phone, but there were none. The next afternoon I was sitting at the nurses' station on the first floor when an elderly Saudi gentleman appeared in front of me clutching what appeared to be several gigantic bags of coins. I indicated my interest and ended up buying a bag of fifty riyals worth. I did not question the reason for this fortuitous happening, but accepted it as a blessing from Allah.

The second interest of the day was the expulsion and deportation from the kingdom of the deputy chief nurse. Now it could not have happened to a better person, for this man was disliked by the company and MOH alike. He was an Arab of some obscure origin who insisted he was British. He was supposedly a qualified nurse administrator, but he had no knowledge of administration or staff management that I could see and did no work at all, spending his time interfering in the wards and making trouble for the nurses.

I never did find out who it was he finally upset enough to get the boot, but he was gone in twenty-four hours with a month's pay and his fare paid. I spent the rest of the day wondering how I could arrange to be fired.

One day in the operating theatre, an English theatre technician was assisting the surgeon. At a particularly trying moment the call to prayer boomed in his ear over the loud speaker, and he said, in a burst of irritation, 'I could do without that.' He was deported within twenty-four hours, lucky that he was not also charged by the religious police with blasphemy or speaking against Islam.

Now I had to start again getting repairs done, this time for the wards of my floor. When I was supposedly being oriented by The Discontented Toad, I had asked her the correct way to order repairs and where I could find the requisition forms. She told me that there were no forms and that I should send the ward servant with a note. These 'servants' were members of the cleaning company's staff but I thought this term awful and re-designated them messengers. I wrote a note asking for repairs to be done and despatched the messenger to the maintenance office. The note bounced back like a boomerang with the messenger attached. I then took it to the office myself, and they said, 'Where is the requisition form?' They showed me the form I was supposed to use, and I took a sample of it back to show D. Toad who, opening a drawer in the desk where she had enough forms to withstand a ten-year siege, said calmly, 'Yes. You must do it in duplicate.' I did so and returned to the office. They said, 'You do not need to do it in duplicate, and you should not bring it here. You must send it to the engineer's office in the basement with your messenger.' After much explanation to the messenger, who in his two years at the hospital had never seen this form, I sent him off. He came back later, with the rebounding form, to tell me that it was not the engineer's department but housing's. Undaunted, I despatched him to the housing office in the compound, complete with form. It took a lot of encouragement to persuade him to go on these trips as he was in mortal terror of displeasing D. Toad, and with just cause. He had not yet got the message that she had been replaced and that it was the done thing to take orders from me. He returned and told me that they said they did not do repairs.

I was now back to square one, having drawn blanks on all my endeavours, but I had not yet given up. While I stood at the nurses' station pondering how I could solve this one, along came a handsome young Saudi, dressed in an immaculately laundered and ironed white *thobe* and red-checked *gutera*, with gold cuff-links at his wrists and a gold stud in his collar: he was the food services director. He said to me, 'Do you need help, Sister?' I could have fallen at his feet and kissed the hem of his garment. He spoke perfect English and understood me far better than Toad Face.

My new ally gave me a phone number to call for repairs. I dialled the number and got someone who spoke no English and who promptly hung up on me. The food director then phoned for me and, after a long conversation, handed me the phone.

'Sister, you shall bring the form to my office.'

'Yes. Gladly. But the reason that I am on the phone is that no-one knows where your office is.'

'It's in front of the workshop.'

'Where is the workshop?'

'It's behind the office.'

'But where is the office?' I said, beginning to feel as though I was starring in a Marx Brothers film.

'It's in front of the workshop.'

'But where is the workshop?'

This time, after a lot of thought, he said, 'It's next to the housing block.'

'But which housing block?' I replied.

It seemed we had reached a stalemate. Not giving up, however, I began again. 'Where do I take the form?'

'To my office.'

'But I do not know where it is.'

My new friend said, 'Give me the form and I will send my messenger to the office with it.'

Three weeks later I had heard nothing more about my repairs, but I am sure that the form arrived, and eventually the repairs were made.

That night I went to the village *souk* in the company bus and, after buying fruit and vegies, the other company staff and I decided that we would try to get

Mustafa to let us stay through prayers so that we could do more shopping afterwards. There was a place outside one of the shops in the street that had a few rough tables and chairs, where the local men sat and had coffee and smoked *hookahs* in the evening. When all the men went off to pray, we sat down and rested.

It was pleasant to be sitting outside in the open, something I had not done since I arrived. There was nowhere to sit in the compound, it would have been frowned upon, and so far it had been far too hot to contemplate. Even at midnight in Medina it was always around forty degrees celsius. When there was a breeze, it was a hot and nasty one, and sometimes the *shimoon* roared out of the desert, foul and searing hot, as though it came from a furnace. I was told that a cooler season did exist and usually began in November, but I found it hard to contemplate. It was now the first week in October and, sitting outside that night for the first time, I felt that it might be just a little, I cannot say cooler, but maybe, less hot.

15 Mosques and marvels

At the end of my fourth week in the kingdom, a trip to Jeddah was scheduled. Jeddah is six hundred kilometres from Medina and too far for a day trip by bus, so it was to be an overnight excursion.

Although I had been told before I came to Saudi Arabia that there was a company bus to take the staff out every weekend to Yanbu or Jeddah, no-one had mentioned that it was not easy, or that it took a long time to get to these places. In my year at KFH I only managed to get away a total of nine times. For a start, you had to have the day off duty. Then the bus had to be scheduled to go, which Roger arranged at his discretion. Sometimes the bus or the driver was broken down, for Mustafa did not like to work on weekends and often took sickies when our day out was due.

The bus left for Jeddah at one o'clock on Thursday after prayers and returned at around ten on Friday evening. To get the extra time off we had to work over-time during the week.

I worked until half past twelve on Thursday and, after a quick change, was at the gate at one o'clock, waiting for Mustafa and his little bus. There were only twelve of us this time. Off we chugged on the five-to-six hour drive, in an atmosphere like that of a bunch of kids just let out of school.

The road south to Jeddah was one of the the kingdom's excellent new highways, part of the total of 18,000 kilometres of main roads built since 1976. It ran from the far north, through Yanbu, down the coast to Jeddah and to the southern regions beyond.

Jeddah was due south past Mecca, which was not, of course, for our unworthy eyes. The road made a wide detour around it, as it did at Medina. At first the ground consisted of stony plains and salty basins, utterly barren country covered with colourless pebbles and flints. There was nothing as far as the horizon, on which a sea of mirage floated. Occasionally a dust devil, or sand goblin, whirled, twirled and danced away over the desolate plain. Further south, around Mecca, the plains gave way to black basalt, volcanic rocks and ridges. Miles and miles of lava beds followed, with pile upon pile of rocks scattered along both sides of the road and among these, here and there, were the remains of old volcanoes.

There were no trees or grass growing anywhere except in the few small oases we passed. Twice we saw a collection of the traditional black Beduin tents, but the only living things we saw were a few camels and the odd hawk rising and falling over the shimmering desert watching for the slightest movement that could signify a meal.

At about two o'clock, Mustafa decided that it was time he ate. Scrawny as he was, he had a great appetite, and nothing kept him from his meals. People told me that in the beginning of his employment with the company, he had been told to charge his meals to them. At the hotel where we stayed in Jeddah, he had subsequently managed to consume one hundred and fifty dollars worth of food in the twenty-four hours of his first sojourn. As the meals are not all that expensive, it was no mean feat. I was filled with admiration for his capacity after hearing this. A man so dedicated to his stomach cannot be all bad. Since Mustafa's monumental eat-in, his carte-blanche at the hotel had been removed from him and he had a food allowance instead. This meant that he now ate at local places, which were very cheap.

Before eating he filled the bus with petrol. I checked the price, and it worked out to be the equivalent of fourteen cents a gallon. Wonderful! Except that this was the one place in the world where it would be of no use to me. By contrast, water, which was sold by the litre bottle, cost sixty-two cents.

The cafe was a dilapidated affair which sat alone in the midst of a bare, empty plain. We had no choice but to eat here or wait until Jeddah, which was too far for me. The owner was Turkish, and he obligingly showed the ladies into a back room, where we were seated at an old deal table on rickety wooden chairs. There was an airconditioner, but it was barely making headway against the heat in this corrugated-iron shed.

The obliging Turk spread our rough table with a flourish of plastic tablecloth and cooked us some kebabs, serving them with salad and the local unleavened bread, which I irreverently called cow flaps. (There was a bigger, leavened type, which I called lavatory seats because their shape made me nostalgic for that item, now missing from my life.) This meal, which was cordon bleu after the hospital tucker, cost me, including two Pepsis, two dollars. It was, into the bargain, delicious, even though we had to do ceaseless battle with the flies to maintain our rights to it. I had brought a heap of munchies and drinks with me on the bus, but I had forgotten about the lack of ladies' facilities in roadside places. By now my need was approaching urgency, so I asked the proprietor what was available. He very kindly led me to his little house, which was across the paddock. There he proudly presented me to his young wife, showed me his baby boy of about ten months and withdrew.

The sweet young wife was thrilled to have a visitor. She would not have had much female company out there in the middle of nowhere, and her husband could never bring his male friends to the house. She showed me the baby and touched my clothes, my hair and skin, lifting my *abeya* and headscarf, feeling the material of my skirt and blouse and the texture of my hair between her fingers and gently stroking my arm and cheek. With my few words of fractured Arabic and a lot of sign language, we had a conversation.

The hut consisted of only one room with a bed and a cupboard. The baby's cot was a cloth hammock slung from the ceiling and within arm's distance of the bed so that it could easily be reached in the night.

High up in the wall was an airconditioner going flat out, being almost entirely defeated by the heat and gaps and cracks. In one corner of the room was a curtain behind which was the cooking equipment, and in the other corner there had been erected a small wooden square which partitioned off the wash house/ablutions centre. This had a hole in the floor for use as a toilet. Above it was a tap that could be turned on to flush it. The floor was cement and on this the man's wife had been in the process of doing the washing when I arrived. This would also have been the place to wash yourself, though there was barely enough room to use the toilet. The entrance door to this bathroom was a rough bit of wood, with many holes and a big gap top, bottom and sides, and there was no way to secure it, but my need was greater than my modesty. Despite its extreme primitiveness, the entire place was spotlessly clean, and I was most grateful for the hospitality shown me.

Just after six that evening we reached Jeddah. It is on the west coast of the Arabian Peninsula and directly on the Red Sea. The heart of the city is on the sea shore, where old wooden boats and men casting nets can be seen, evoking scenes dating back before biblical times. Close offshore is a coral reef that is a diver's paradise and runs all the way up the west coast. The old town, which was once enclosed by walls, is over two thousand years old. Jeddah long ago attracted merchants from Persia, India, Syria, Egypt and Oman, who eventually settled there, giving rise to its cosmopolitan atmosphere.

In 1969 there were only six cars in Jeddah. Today it is a mass of traffic and roads. All the roads, freeways and the new city have been built since 1973 and are exceedingly modern. The new city has been built around the old, completely encapsulating it, and where it was once on the sea shore, it is now separated from the sea by a six-lane super highway and several rows of polished new buildings, all built on land reclaimed from the sea.

The company had an arrangement with an Egyptian-managed hotel in Jeddah, which provided us with accommodation at reduced rates: hotels in the Middle East are among the most expensive in the world. Once inside the hotel, it was possible to discard your *abeya* and even headscarf, as long as you maintained a modest form of dress. It now felt strange without them.

The hotel clientele was a mixture of Saudis, some with their women trailing along behind them in full *purdah*; other Middle Eastern businessmen, and a few foreign workers and businessmen. Downstairs there were, naturally, no bars, but there were comfortable lounges and sitting-rooms. I went downstairs to join the group who were going in the company bus to the International Market on the other side of the town. This turned out to be a modern and westernised shopping centre, with jewellery, electrical, clothes and food shops; the latter selling pizzas, hamburgers and ice cream. I bought some teach-yourself Arabic lessons, and a stereo, radio-cassette ghetto blaster. The king has a policy to provide his people with goods at reasonable prices and, as tax is also considered immoral, there is no import tax levied on goods brought into the country. The cassette player provided wonderful entertainment in my deprived life, but the radio was spasmodic. Sometimes I could get the BBC and hear the news, but mostly there was just a great deal of static and crackling. The news coming in to Saudi Arabia is heavily censored, and I believe that sometimes the broadcasting stations were deliberately scrambled. I also bought a wardrobe of head scarves; long, rectangular white or black pieces of fabric, some of which had edges decorated prettily with embroidery, beads, sequins and gold and silver thread. They were long enough to go over the head, and around the neck with the end drawn across the face.

We had been in the centre only an hour when the call to prayer sounded, all the shops shut, and everyone went off to pray, except the infidels who sat on the seats around the fountains in the arcades, and waited for prayer time to finish.

I saw the *matawain* – the religious police – go through. They banged on the shop windows with their heavy camel sticks and shouted '*salaat!*' – prayer. The sticks they carried were of knotted wood and were used to beat anyone they considered to be offending Islam, as were their camel whips. I heard of foreign women workers who had been whacked for showing too much arm or leg, and I saw them hit Filipino nurses on two occasions. Once, outside the door of the compound shop where they sometimes used to watch people go in and out, a girl was beaten around the head and shoulders for having her hair not completely covered by her scarf. Another nurse had her face slapped twice because, as she walked through the door the wind blew her *abeya* and showed her dress and ankle. *Matawain* were like vigilantes and were very much feared. You never knew who they were. Unlike the regular police, they did not wear uniforms but dressed in the usual Saudi *thobe* and *ghutera*. I was told that they had many spies, as did the regular espionage outfit under the control of the Ministry of the Interior, and that you could assume that in our hospital an average of one in five Saudis, or Arabs (for they employed others besides Saudis), would be a spy of some sort. Westerners in particular, live in fear of the *matawain*.

In the morning I found another like-minded soul, in the form of an Indian woman doctor, and she and I set off to see the old town. The hotel desk person told us that it would be seemly for us to go alone, as long as we wore *abeyas* and head-coverings. We went by taxi to the main *souk*, passing along the wide carriageway beside the foreshore, known as the Corniche, which runs for miles along the edge of the sea, some of it on reclaimed land. The king's palace is on this road, facing the sea, as well as a large and beautiful mosque, parks and recreation areas. It was Friday, and there were many families out enjoying themselves. Although Jeddah was more liberal towards foreign women, I noticed that the local women still wore complete *purdah*. Some of them, however, did not cover their entire faces, as they did in Medina, but left their eyes visible, wearing a veil with an open slit over the eye area. Combined with the pretty scarf edging wrapped around their faces and necks, it was highly decorative.

Crossing the Corniche, we walked through the arcade of a great, modern block of shops called The Queen's Building and, emerging from its back door, we stepped out of the modern Jeddah and into the old, like *Alice Through the Looking Glass*. There were no hideous concrete office blocks, no traffic or super highways, but narrow, winding sheltered lanes with soft sand underfoot. There was no room here, in these shadowy, shuttered depths for cars: you now had to go on foot or by donkey among the labyrinth of houses, shops and mosques. Apart from the chatter and haggling, there was only the soft footfall of sandals on sand or cobblestones. Here were the picturesque, old, traditional houses and shops, large and imposing, a blend of Turkish and Egyptian architecture using local materials and adapted to suit the climate.

My companion and I wandered for an hour or more among the covered alleys of the *souk* and little lanes of the old town; shaded by the large and densely packed houses, rejoicing in the simple pleasure of being on our own and at large. There was a mystical feel within those ancient walls. Every now and then we came across mosques of obvious antiquity, some with interior water cisterns and wells, from which the people used to fetch their water in the days before the oil money provided water desalination plants. As it was Friday most of the shops in the *souk* were closed and there were few people around. At about half past eleven the call to prayer began and the *mezzuin* called 'Allah wakhbar', or God is great, from the six mosques of the old town, and the call reverberated among the ancient walls and buildings. We sat down under the famous tree, once the only tree in Jeddah, in front of The House with the Tree, on a wooden bench which had been built around it. Here there was a small cobbled square into which ran half a dozen little cobbled lanes. On one side of the square was an old mosque, with a quaint minaret which changed from hexagonal to cylindrical and decreased in width as it rose higher; it had a rickety and not altogether straight look about it. A rough hewn, coral stone staircase ascended one side of the mosque, up which the men went to their prayers.

Lunch at the hotel was in the form of the traditional Arab feast. A huge, circular steel cooking pot, big enough in which to boil a whole sheep, contained just that. There was a succession of smaller steel pots, containing vegetables, rice and wheat dishes. Many dishes included eggplant, delicious in the various ways it was prepared. Next came salads, sweet dishes and dishes of small hors-d'oeuvre, such as pickles and salamis. Most of the sweets were very sticky and sickly looking cakes and confections.

The victuals were washed down with pots of tea, or you could order soft drinks or 'cocktails' from the 'drinks menu'. No effort had been spared in the effort to delude the guest into believing that this was the same as a western hotel. The drinks menu described cocktails with wonderful, imaginative names and long lists of ingredients: none of which was alcohol. Perhaps they thought that by the time you had read to the end of the list, it might have slipped your mind that there was no demon drink in them. Then there was the infamous 'Saudi Champagne', which consisted of Perrier water and apple juice. I was not fooled. When you come from a place where hotel is synonymous with booze, rather than bed, you are not deluded for one moment by such tactics.

After a fabulous repast, I retired to the lounge and pretended to read a book, while I observed the comings and goings of the hotel guests; the sheiks sweeping in with a following from the harem, a gaggle of bundles in black, dutifully and demurely gliding along behind, and businessmen of many nationalities, in twos and threes. It seemed true that Jeddah was indeed cosmopolitan. I had even been told, by one of the hospital staff who had previously worked in Jeddah, that she had come face to face with Idi Amin in a hospital here. She said that he was the most enormous man she had ever seen; huge across the shoulders and chest, and very tall. He had brought one of his wives to the hospital for treatment – that is, one that he had, so far, not killed and eaten. When no-one else would grant refuge to this monster of depravity, he was given sanctuary by Saudi Arabia because he is one of the brotherhood of Islam.

At five o'clock that evening, the hospital group assembled in the hotel foyer and, once more under the tender care of Mustafa, we set off back into captivity, another five hours driving away. Clearing the outskirts of the town, I noticed the airport to one side. There are two separate airports, one of which is expressly for the Guests of God, the pilgrims, over one million of whom arrive by air each year in Jeddah at the time of the *Haj*.

As dusk fell we were again out among the basalt and lava plains and old volcanoes, and in the twilight a full moon rose above a craggy mountain ridge. It hung there suspended, just above the mountains, silhouetting their ragged edges and looking surrealistic and lovely in the greenish-grey light.

At the friendly Turk's we stopped once more for kebabs and salad. This time though, as it was dark and no-one else was there, we all sat together outside at wooden tables and chairs. (Imagine that – men and women together!) There was a cool breeze blowing from the direction of the coast, and sitting there in the balmy air, miles from anywhere, it was not hard to believe that everything was normal and that the hospital was just a bad dream.

At eleven o'clock we arrived back at the compound gate. There was a scramble for *abeyas* and headscarves, which had been left off until now, and it was once more back into the fold.

On later visits to Jeddah I spent my time exploring the old town. I also found that in the evening, when there were large crowds of local women in twos and threes out shopping, I could go about on my own, as long as I wore my coverings and behaved discreetly. The atmosphere of the old town changed at night and the lanes, lit with gas lamps, took on a hauntingly exotic colour. The shops put up their shutters and spilled their goods out onto the narrow alleys; bales and bales of brilliant coloured cloth, open bags of aromatic spices, jars of incense and henna. Itinerant sellers hawked their wares; the sandal maker, the knife sharpener, and the seller of such things as toothbrushes made from a stick of the Datum tree – the traditional way for Arabs to clean their teeth. The gold shops were dazzling. Although some of them were tumbledown and decrepit, they had a king's ransom sprayed across their tatty walls; baubles, bangles, beads, body ornaments and girdles straight from the Arabian Nights. So extravagant were some of these great girdles and necklaces, often used as bride prices, that you would have presumed them to have been Woolworth specials, if you had not known better.

At the rear of The House with the Tree, I discovered a cafe where it was possible for foreigners to go in groups. The cafe was in an open courtyard, with high overhead a covering of cloth, like a lofty Beduin tent, and was open on all sides to the breeze. Inside it was furnished with low, carpeted benches, couches and cushions on the floor. The couches and benches had bolsters to put under your elbow and on which you reclined to eat and drink, definitely an acquired habit. If men were present it was always presumed that the females were their wives. Exception was made for foreign women to eat in public places in Jeddah, and unless the religious police came along and asked to see our papers – if caught even shopping in the company of a man not one's husband, the sentence could be three days in gaol and eighty lashes – there was no problem. It would have been impossible at Medina. There were so few of us that everyone knew that none of us were spouses, and there were no restaurants outside the walls.

16 I become Sid Vicious

The next morning, after a six o'clock rising, I was terribly tired. I needed much more sleep now than I did at home, owing to a combination of the hours, the six-day week, and the oppressive heat. I sometimes wondered if I slept so much in order to escape. I now could sleep in the afternoon and after work, and I regularly slept for ten hours on my day off.

That day, to my great excitement, I received a letter from my family at home. I had sent sarcastic messages to them, asking if they had been afflicted with brachial palsy and making heavy threats to cut them out of my will and deed the loot collected in my lifetime to the cats' home. It had taken all this time for my first letter to reach home and a letter from my mother to be returned. It was like a visitation from another planet. My mother wrote about a day spent at the beach house of relatives, catching big blue crabs, cooking and eating them on the sand. It made me feel terribly homesick and so far removed from all such simple pleasures. I was filled with longing and yearned to be there.

To take my mind off this, as soon as I finished work I did a load of washing in my wonderful new machine. It was very slow, for it took two hours to do one load and there must surely have been something wrong with it. For all that, I sat on the end of the bath enthralled, watching the washing going around and around through its little window, until I took stock of myself and thought, What ever have I been reduced to that I now find my entertainment in watching the washing in progress? I made up my mind to get a television, no matter what the cost. (After I got it I found that there was not a lot of difference between the washing machine and what the local television stations passed off as entertainment.)

The excitement for the next day was the arrival of some new furniture for the compound housing. This had been ordered by MOH, chosen from European mail order catalogues. It was unassembled, and the pieces were packed in boxes that were stacked in mountainous heaps all around the recreation centre. It was supposedly allocated to people according to the size of their units but, as there was not enough to go around, it went to those whom the authorities felt should have it. I filled out a form and was told I was entitled to three dining chairs, one table, a coffee table, a television cupboard, a bed and bedside cupboard. I took my form to the housing supervisor, my potential friend, and I do not know if that is the reason or not, but I was the only company person who ever received any.

At four o'clock the same day I had a phone call to say that my furniture would be delivered in half an hour, that some workmen would come to assemble it in my flat, and that this would take about an hour. I went to my flat to wait for it. At five o'clock I had another call asking if I was ready for it. I said yes. (I had only been waiting for an hour.) At half past five it arrived, complete with two cheerful Sudanese. All the items on the list were there except the bedside cupboard, which was signed out to me but never did present itself. It must have been syphoned off in transit, a common occurrence.

The large wooden boxes were dumped on the floor, taking up the entire free space in the flat. The Sudanese gents, thinly disguised as the assembly team, discovered that they needed tools for this operation, and one took himself off to get them, while the other sat down on the couch to scrutinise me, the door wide open all the while. I do not know why he stayed; perhaps he thought I needed company or the furniture needed his protection. The first one failed to re-appear. Eventually I offered the remaining one the use of my trusty hammer and screwdriver. It was no use. He did not want my tools; either that or he could not work without his mate.

We sat together for another hour or so until, in order to get rid of him, I said I was going to the shop and that they should return tomorrow with their tools. After much discussion, we agreed (I think) on four o'clock the next day.

My new friend and his accomplice arrived promptly at four the next day, and this time they had brought not only a hammer and screwdriver but also reinforcements in the form of another Sudanese. They took apart all the boxes and made a terrific mess and, after a respectable interval, one actually began to apply the screwdriver to various bits of wood. The other two seated themselves comfortably on the lounge and watched him. Occasionally the more lively of the two jumped up and leaped about the room examining my personal belongings, perusing and fingering the contents of my jewel box, passing my framed photographs around to the others for their comments, interrogating me on my life and relatives and asking some most intimate questions. Now and then the others joined him in these innocent and guileless entertainments.

After one and three-quarter hours of this, I was getting hungry and sleepy. Judging by the progress being made, I could see that the estimated hour for the assembly was going to stretch into a week. By now the first screwer, having exhausted himself, had been relieved, and he took his turn at sitting and watching. At this stage it occurred to them that they needed more tools and, so saying, they cheerily took themselves off, leaving me with chaos in the only living area of my one-roomed flat. They had dismantled my old bed and left the pieces across the corridor where I had to climb over it to get to the bathroom; it was too heavy for me to move it. The new bed was strewn about the place but unassembled. Likewise, the dining table was in bits and pieces; they had only finished the television cabinet and as I did not have a TV, it was not a lot of use.

At eight o'clock I was still sitting there in my uniform waiting for their return. I finally gave up and, picking my way about in no small danger to my limbs in all the clutter, I made my bed on the mattress on the floor in the only spare space I could find and went to sleep.

Four days later nothing had changed, and I was still waiting, less and less patiently, for their return. On the fifth day I gave up and went to ask the housing supervisor where they were. He was aghast to hear that I was sleeping on the floor and said they would be there the next day. They did not arrive that day, but I think they came the day after, while I was in the bath, judging from the concerto that was played upon the doorbell. I ignored it. I was not having that lot in my place while my ablutions were in progress. The following day they came back and, after two and a half hours, succeeded in putting my bed and table together. After that, I never saw my Sudanese workmen again.

I was not going to push my luck any further. I set to work on the furniture myself and managed badly to bang the rest of it together. The coffee table had a permanent list to port (or was it starboard?) and two of the dining chairs were for ornamentation only. I never dared sit on them. At long last I was equipped and furnished.

The water in the housing and the hospital was desalinated salt water that came from huge plants located on the coast and was piped to Medina. It tasted putrid, was as tough as old leather and stuck to your teeth if you were brave enough to drink it. The alternative was to drink bottled water at sixty cents a litre. Once a week I used to fill the bath and add a liberal dose of any kind of oil I could find, mineral or vegetable. Then I would sit in it up to my neck in an effort to soften my hide. After a while I started doing things to my hair. I tried all the coloured rinses on the shelf in the shop, starting at one end and working my way down the line, every few weeks trying another colour. It was great fun now that I no longer had the prospect of having to face people with it. It helped to relieve the boredom of my existence and, as no-one ever saw my hair, what did it matter? Other women must have done the same thing too, judging from the range in the shop. I was in succession burgundy, copper, light blonde, black, dark chestnut and more. Then I decided to experiment with a perm. There was a Filipino kitchen worker who supplemented her meagre wages by fixing people's hair. I would not have braved her somewhat suspect ministrations if I had had to show the results to the world but, as it was, I happily let her do her worst with a perm. And that is just what she did. When I showed it to the British girls they said I looked like Sid Vicious. It stood out all around my head in a sort of wiry frizz, even with my scarf tightly tied over it, and it also went a violent shade of orange. I decided then to let my hair grow and did not have it cut for the rest of the time I was there.

I discovered henna, a powder made from the leaves and shoots of the Egyptian privet and sold by the scoop from a hessian bag. It is a wonderful conditioner and is widely used by Saudi women to colour and condition their hair, and many, particularly the Bedu, used it to decorate their hands, feet and sometimes their faces, painting it on with a small brush or a twig in intricate patterns that lasted until they washed it off. The older men also use it to dye their beards red, which they thought to be attractive.

In my chats with Mercy, the hairdresser, I discovered that she was employed by a small company who was contracted to supply the kitchen workers to the hospital. I would not have believed anyone could be worse off than the cleaners, but then I heard how Mercy lived. She was billeted in a village house rented by her company. There were twenty women in the house, which had five bedrooms and one bathroom and kitchen, and no furniture; they slept on mattresses on the floor and ate on the floor. They had not been paid for months and some of them had not been paid at all. There are laws to protect workers, but there are not enough people employed to enforce them, and it is not easy for workers to get to an office of the Labour Court to complain.

17 Florence of Arabia

By now, having got to know my way around, and a few helpful Saudis, I felt more secure: I had the system working for me. I was nice to some pretty repulsive people in order to try to take care of the patients and nurses who were my responsibility, and I found some lovely Arabs.

There are two kinds: the town Arabs and the Bedu – the nomads. The Bedu have evolved from their lives in the desert into a tough, proud people. They consider themselves the Lords of the Earth and the Chosen of God, as it was their land and their race that produced the last prophet. At heart all Saudis retain the ideals of the Bedu, who has been immortalised in fiction as a law unto himself; obstinately his own master. The truth is not far from the fiction. He takes his gun where he wants (even on an aircraft) and would come into the hospital festooned with bandoliers of bullets and swinging a rifle. His women sometimes mean less to him than his animals. I often saw the goat riding in the front of the utility with the master, the wife/wives in the open back in the heat, dust and flies. The Bedu drives where he wants on the road and scorns traffic rules and road signs. He treats road rules and police with equal contempt. Once when I threatened to call the resident policeman to an unruly Bedu, he stood his ground and said, 'Why should I be afraid of him? He is just a man like I am.' He believes that all men are equal and calls the king by his first name when he meets him. There is no work ethic in Bedu culture. When a Bedu comes to a town to live, he will not work with his hands, which he believes to be demeaning: a man is honoured or dishonoured by the work he does and honour is more important to him than anything else. The only gainful jobs which he will take are non-manual ones such as driving. But I admired the way in which the Bedu steadfastly refused to bow to western ways and be subdued by a supposedly superior civilisation.

Besides getting to know the people, I was becoming accustomed to the way of life in Saudi Arabia. I had got used to addressing everyone as sister or brother. This was strange at first. It took me long years of hard labour and toil to be entitled to be called sister, I reflected, and now I had to use it for the cleaners and kitchen-maids as well as the Bedu. In Australia brothers are in religious orders and sisters are either registered nurses or nuns. In Saudi Arabia it is an Islamic form of address and signifies that everyone is equal, brother and sister, under Allah. It also helped the locals to eliminate our surnames, which they found difficult, for they called us sister or brother followed by our first name. I became Sister Lydia.

On the wards I encountered little of the gross sexism I had been told to expect from patients. Only a few times was I treated with contempt. Once, as I happened along, a patient who was getting very stroppy with the nurses, waved his hand imperiously in my direction and shouted, 'You! Come here!' I turned to the interpreter who was at my side (even though it was obvious that this patient spoke English) and said, 'Tell this man that as far as I am concerned a gentleman does not address a woman in this manner,' and stalked off. The next day when I came to that ward, the stroppy patient produced a box of chocolates for me with an abject apology. We discussed his problems and he was thereafter a model patient and always treated me like a duchess.

From the start I had begun acquiring a few fractured words of Arabic. It greatly pleased the Arabs to hear me try, and they did not think it sacrilegious for a *Nasrani* to speak of their God. They do believe that we have the same God, but that we, The people of the Book (the term for Christians and Jews – monotheists), are misguided. They believe that Jesus Christ was a great prophet and accord him due reverence. In Egypt I heard people say, 'peace be upon him', after saying his name, the same as they do after saying the name of their most revered prophet, Mohommed (peace be upon him), who was the founder of their religion. I would have been joyfully welcomed into the fold if I had wanted to profess Islam. Several of the more devout brothers came to tell me of their religious beliefs in the hope of converting me, and the *Imam* – the religious leader – brought me books and cassette tapes about Islam when he heard that I was prepared to listen.

I struggled, however, with more than simple greetings. Arabic is a rich and flexible language, wonderfully expressive in poetry, and spoken it is beautiful and lyrical. I loved to listen to it, especially the readings from the Koran on television, but it has sounds that English does not have, which makes it more difficult for us to learn. There is, for example *ach*, which sounds like you are clearing your throat. And *kh*, which sounds like a gargle. But if it is not easy to learn to speak and is the very devil to try to write, comparisons cannot be made with the English alphabet, because Arabic has twenty-eight letters – all consonants and no vowels. Arriving at the end of our alphabet we have *x y z*; Arabic ends with *ha, wow, ya*. It is written right to left or backwards to our way of thinking. Reading a book, you start at what to us would be the back cover and the last line and progress forward from there.

The spoken language is very difficult to learn, and I did not get as much chance as I would have liked to practise it, as there were only a few native English speakers at the hospital and most Arabic speakers who had some English wanted to practise with us. That only left the Bedu patients and the Saudis, who would not condescend to learning an infidel tongue, and they were not a lot of fun to chat with.

I got on quite well with the Arabic lessons on the television and from there mastered the alphabet and then began to be able to pick out words from notices and signs about the place. This I found surprising, because I had always looked at written Arabic and thought that it was so pretty but that I would never be able to decipher it. Slowly it began to fall into place. Spelling, however, is a movable feast. Arabic is a phonetic language and a large number of Arabic people are illiterate, so no-one cares much about how things are spelt (this would please a certain member of my family whose spelling has always been erratic). All signs are written in Arabic, and even after you have learned to say the word, it is still not possible to read it until you learn the script. Letters arriving from other countries had to have the address translated into Arabic before they could be delivered. This was one of the reasons that so much mail got lost: it was either translated wrongly or, if it could not be read, was abandoned. A tourist industry would change things, but the rulers of the country do not want the corruption of tourists and, even if they did, they have little to offer. No-one in his or her right mind would consider going to Saudi Arabia for a holiday. Millions of pilgrims visit, but they come to see the holy shrines and to fulfil their religious duties, not for the beauties and pleasures of the country.

The conservatism of the Saudis is evident in more than their wish to be spared the pollution of infidel tourists. Punishment for wrongdoing seems mediæval; today in Saudi Arabia the right hand is still cut off for stealing. This is done in the traditional way, lopped off with a large sword in the public square with the victim kneeling before the public executioner, and the stump is plunged into boiling fat to seal the wound and stop bleeding and infection. They say that the fat hurts more than the amputation does. I saw several men during my time in the country who were minus a hand.

One of the male nurses on my floor, an obliging Palestinian named Anwar, had gone into Medina one Friday on his day off and bought a television and video for me. Islam prohibits pictures and sculptures, restricts books and there are no cinemas or other public entertainments, so that television, videos and stereos are big business and very popular. The TV programmes were awful and the video films very bland and innocuous, but it (sometimes) beat watching the washing go round. There were two television channels, one in Arabic and one in English. The Arabic programmes seemed to be largely religious, with long sessions of religious discussion and talks. They both began at five and went until eleven in the evening. Both programmes began the same way. First came the national anthem, a rousing affair sounding a lot like a German drinking song. This was followed by a recitation from the Koran in Arabic by a fellow with a deep, resonant voice. Immediately afterwards on the English channel there was a translation of the verse in English. Then came the entertainment: old American shows, heavily censored and edited, or part of a serial, slightly out of context. Every instance of the slightest hint of intimacy between males and females, for example, a father kissing a child, was deleted. Sometimes there was very little left or what did remain was so disjointed as to be incomprehensible. *The Muppet Show* was banned. The star of the show, the glamorous Miss Piggy was *persona non grata* in Saudi Arabia.

Peak-hour viewing from six to seven was *Sesame Street*. I got quite fond of it and can still sing along (in private, of course) with the title song whenever I hear it. At nine there was the news in French, and at half past nine, the news in English. This was watched by everyone in the compound, not for the news, but for its humour, which was unintentional but hilarious. It seemed as though anyone could get to read the news in English on television. There were many different announcers and their only qualifications seemed to be that they had a friend or a relative in the station. They had atrocious accents – some were almost unintelligible – and mixed up words and their meanings comically. One announcer said the politicians were flustering their policies and that Gorbachev and Reagan should scrape their differences; one that the weather in Europe was causing cows on the highways; and another that so-and-so was accused of deprivity. A really all-weather word 'deprivity'. It seemed to me that if announcers couldn't think of the word they made one up. The best howler I heard was a news reader trying to say pomegranate groves. He had about ten goes and never did get it out.

The strange thing was that I met many Saudis who had been educated at Oxford and spoke perfect English. Why could they not have found some among them to read the news in English if they wanted to broadcast it?

Because there were no commercials to fill in empty spaces, there were frequent announcements of the next day's prayer times for all regions in the kingdom. These varied according to the sun's position and are different each day. They gave the flight times and arrivals for all planes entering and leaving the kingdom (the reason for which I could not fathom) and the opening times of the pharmacies in each town of all the provinces.

The programmes were always stopped during prayer times, and the call to prayer and some prayers played during this interval. As they stopped for the call to prayer in all the main cities – Medina, Mecca, Riyadh and Dharan – and as they were all at different times and as there were two calls to prayer for each district during each evening's viewing time, making eight in all, it did not leave a lot of television time. The programmes were not stopped and started again after prayers but cut, so that what was missed was gone forever.

The news always started with the doings of the king and the other important members of the royal family for that day and in that order. There would be minutes of film showing the king greeting visitors or attending a function, and kissing guest after guest, always to the accompaniment of a Strauss waltz. If no film were available, his photo would be shown on the screen, and his doings for that day read out. This took up at least half of the time allotted for the news. News of the world followed and took about five minutes; it was highly censored. World War III could have started, but it would still have had to take a back seat to the king's doings for the day. He is the boss in the old-fashioned way.

Saudis are very keen on soccer and other sport, so that was usually reasonably well reported, although no women competing were ever shown. (Women in Saudi are not permitted to go to sporting events, let alone compete.) The weather followed, taking one minute flat. There's not a lot of weather in Arabia. It hardly ever changed. It was either hot or warm and rained rarely.

At the completion of the news on Friday, immediately before the weather, the executions would be announced. The names of those who had been put down and where and why were given in a matter of fact statement. It went as follows: 'The Minister of the Interior issued a statement today that the government of King Fahid Ibn Abdul Aziz Al Saud is as determined as ever to to maintain peace and security and to curb crime and strike hard on criminals. The Minister of the Interior announces today the execution in Jeddah of Mohommed Ibn – for killing, and Ibrahim Ibn – for helping, and in Riyadh the execution of Abdul Ibn – for killing and the wife, Fatma – for helping, ten years in prison and seventy-nine lashes. And here are the temperatures for today.'

Most people did not watch much television. A small library of videos was available for company staff. Supplied by Arabian Health, they were pirated from American television, and were of poor quality and full of commercials. Sometimes I enjoyed the commercials more than the films, as they gave a glimpse of the real world out there, of consumerism and advertising that looked so attractive because I could no longer be part of them. Because of censorship the films were pretty harmless. Disney featured heavily and even that was cut about. On television they even censored the children's cartoons like *Tom and Jerry* as well as *The Three Stooges*, which was at times shown on a Friday as a special treat. In one episode Mo was falling about, in his usual manner, in a dressmaker's shop where there was a female dressmaker's dummy. He fell onto it and grasped it, or so I deduced from what happened next, as that part was cut out.

My radio and television reception was not too bad. Those who lived next to the mosque got very little or no reception at all. There was something in there which interfered with sound waves, possibly the massive amplifier used for the call to prayer. Although the *mezzuin* actually does a live show, the call is greatly amplified. Even seven minutes walk away where I lived it could be heard distinctly above the airconditioner's rattle and hum in my flat.

The MOH staff got their videos from Medina if they were Muslim and, if not, they organised it so that someone brought films from the Philippines when returning from leave. The Muslim films were all in Arabic and either religious or Egyptian soap-operas. There was a good deal of swapping and borrowing of videos among the hospital staff. They were the only source of entertainment in the compound, with the exception of the Filipino female parties, which were really just eating contests (at which I did very well). The girls were very fond of having big cook-ups and didn't need much of an excuse. They were, naturally, for women only. I got invited to them all, and I had to go to most so that I did not hurt anyone's feelings. For people who loved to cook they made some gruesome food. Their main meat or pasta dishes were fine, but they adored masses of desserts in lurid colours, which tasted as livid as they looked, and they made huge cakes with great glaring slabs of icing resembling coloured cement.

After this they expected me to dance with women! I danced, but I drew the line firmly and finally at singing and in the end they gave up trying to get me to sing for them. How lucky they were and what a narrow escape they had. They all sing, and in public too, at the drop of a hat, and fail to understand that some people simply cannot put two notes together in tune. I failed the test for the school choir when I was twelve and have never warbled a note in public since.

One day at the beginning of this month of *Jumal al Thani*, the temperature dropped below forty degrees and it was officially declared to be winter. The clock was altered to daylight saving time, for what purpose I could not see. There was not much change in the time of sunrise or sunset. I think it was just another attempt to keep up with the Joneses; the west had daylight saving, why not the Arabs? The Saudi men now put on their winter woollies and at the hospital up the road the pool was drained and cleaned and left empty, even though the temperature was often over forty and most of the expats were still gasping from the heat.

As I have said, all Saudis wear *thobes*, an elongated shirt which reaches to the ground; it is a testimony to the equality of men that they all dress the same, even the king. In the summer they wore the white *thobe*, which differed only from one to the other by its cleanliness and elegance. Some were mass produced for sale to the Bedu and the less discriminating: the town Arab of means had his tailored. At a distance they all looked the same, but on closer inspection some were beautifully cut, with mandarin collars in which two gold studs were worn, and well-finished cuffs that sported plain gold or fancy cuff links. Sometimes they would have cuffs and collars that were embroidered at the edges with delicate designs in white. On a dark handsome man this was very fetching.

In the winter, the *thobes* were made of woollen or worsted material in a light grey or brown. The elegant had them tailored, like a traditional three-piece suit from the best suiting material. Some of them appeared to have the best Saville Row tailors – and they probably did. This was great from the waist up, but when you looked down, it was a surprise to see this dazzling maleness ending in a skirt.

On really cold days, when it got down to thirty or so, a cape or cloak, the Saudi overcoat, called a *mishlah*, was added. This was a full and flowing, sleeveless garment with slits for the arms. It could appear most impressive, like the pictures you see of the Arab sheik galloping out on his trusty charger, with cloak flowing behind in the wind. The cloaks were made in dark woollen material, the more expensive being trimmed with gold braid. Saudi men cover their heads at all times, either with a red-and-white checked or plain white *gutera*. The colour seems to be only personal preference, although some say they wear the white ones in the hot weather because they are cooler. But the Bedu in the Medina district only ever wore red. On top of the *gutera* they wear a black double-twisted circle, the *aghal*, which looks like rope and which the expats rudely call fan belts. It holds the *gutera* on and was originally part of a camel rope or whip, much the same as the stockmen at home use a piece of stockwhip around their hats. Under the *gutera* they wear a stiff embroidered round white skull cap: the *Hadji* cap that you see worn in other countries by Muslims who have made the pilgrimage. On their feet they almost always wear sandals made from camel leather in a classical style with a thong around the big toe, except in the winter, when some of the nattier wear socks and expensive imported leather shoes. Most men carry prayer or worry beads, which are like a rosary; some are made of semi-precious stones or minerals, expensive and beautiful. Some carry a fine camel stick, which reminded me of the swagger-sticks carried by the dandies in nineteenth century England.

The women, although they all look the same when covered from head to toe with the black of *purdah*, could cause some surprise when they took their covers off in the hospital. It was a shock to discover that underneath they were mostly clad in bright colours and shiny materials. This applied to the patients I saw who were mostly Bedu but, in the capital and in Jeddah, I believe the wealthy wore the latest fashions under the *abeya*, which would only ever be seen by other women and their husbands. The Bedu still wear long dresses with long sleeves in old-fashioned designs, and they love glitter and sparkle. Their dresses look like evening gowns. Even the little girls are dressed like this. They do not go into *purdah* until they are about eleven or twelve so I used to see them visiting the hospital in their bows, ribbons and sequins. They looked so ornate and gorgeous. The town Arab women wore western clothes under their *abeyas*, but with long sleeves, and skirts to the ground, because this was Medina. They all wore their hair long and braided or pinned up, and lots of jewellery, much of it gold, as this is the traditional way of investing money. I was surprised at how fair-skinned some of the Saudis and other Middle Easterners are, especially the women whose skin never sees the sun. The Bedu are all quite dark, but the town Arabs vary considerably. Some are absolutely shiny black, from intermarriage or breeding with slaves from Africa. Many are fair-skinned and green-eyed, as are some Syrians, who often have bright red hair and blue or green eyes and look more Irish than Middle Eastern. In the hospital we had all types of Middle Eastern people; occasionally you saw a real Sinbad the Sailor in a very full bell-shaped *thobe*, with a round fat turban wound around and around that rose up to a peak in the centre. Others wore Turkish dress: loose baggy trousers, big floppy shirt hanging down over them and pointed turned-up-toed slippers. They looked like figures out of my childhood story books, and I was enchanted.

I wore mostly long caftans under my *abeya*, for even when taking it off in the hotel in Jeddah, for example, it was necessary to be covered adequately.

One day in mid-November, on one of my precious Fridays off, I noticed for the first time that it was decidedly cooler, so I turned off the airconditioner and opened the windows. I guess that it had been gradually getting cooler for a while, but when it happens so slowly it takes time for it to register. This day was suddenly quite different. Through the open window came a light, spring-like breeze that stirred and fluttered my bright blue curtains. The sunlight shone over the window ledge and, no longer my mortal enemy, lay in a bright, friendly pool on my feet. It was almost like being outside, enjoying the beauties of nature. I imagined that the Bird Man of Alcatraz felt like this when his birds came to his window, bringing with them the freedom of the outside world.

Without the racket of the airconditioner I could hear the twittering of little birds and the cooing of the pigeons that were strutting up and down along the roof edge opposite. With the windows open and a good breeze blowing through them my flat felt lighter and more spacious. I felt again, as I had felt on the roof tops of Katmandu many years before, free and light-hearted.

In through the window came the inevitable voice of the *mezzuin* calling the faithful to prayer, '*Allah Wakhbar*, God is most great.'

18 A patient interlude

Achmed, a small Beduin boy of about eight, was admitted to our hospital with a large ulcer on his leg, the result of a burn from the cooking fire. His father was a driver in Medina and the family had settled near the town. A consultation form was sent to the plastic surgeon requesting his services for a possible skin graft. Little Achmed had also been born with a severe deformity of both arms, which looked rather like the malformations caused by thalidomide. Both arms ended near the elbow, and on the ends were the rudiments of hands with a couple of finger-like attachments. Achmed could use these with reasonable ability to feed himself. At first he was very shy and kept his arms hidden in the sleeves of his *thobe*, but as he realised that his deformity did not matter to us he began to use them as normal. I gave him some pencils and paper to play with and discovered that he could use his hands well enough to make drawings. He enjoyed it, drawing for hours at a time. Islam does not permit many children's toys; pictures and dolls which are considered to be conducive to idolatry are forbidden, and books are not encouraged unless they are religious or educational. I asked if he went to school, and he said, *La, Mumkin* – 'No, it is not possible.' 'Would you like to go?' I asked. *Aiya. Aywah!* 'Oh, yes!' he replied.

Later I asked his father why he did not go to school and he said, 'It is the will of Allah. He is different from the other boys. It would be hard for him.'

I looked at Achmed's bright, little face, intelligence shining from his eyes, and I said, 'But this boy has a good brain. He will not be able to work with his hands as you do, so he must have an education to enable him to work with his brain instead.' His father merely smiled and said, 'If God wills it.'

When the plastic surgeon, a British trained Indian, examined Achmed, he was very keen to do some surgery to improve the boy's hands and arms, but the father refused to allow it saying, 'This is the way Allah made him. It is the will of Allah. *Allah Wakhbar* – God is most great!'

In Saudi Arabia I encountered The Watcher – a phenomenon new to me. The Watcher was a person who was admitted with a patient to watch and take care of them. In reality, Watchers policed the nurses and doctors, the other patients and any medical drama they could get near. Generally they were thoroughgoing nuisances who did little to ease the nurse's burden and much to weigh them down. In theory Watchers spent twenty-four hours of the day by the patient's bed. They were provided with enormous reclining armchairs which made adequate beds at night, grand chairs by day and terrific obstacles to bedside care. With hospital meals thrown in, it made a fine holiday. The reason for their presence was the idea, not all that mistaken in the case of KFH, that the loved one would not be given adequate attention by strangers. But far from spending the entire day ministering to the needs of their dear relative, many spent their time wandering about the wards and hospital in search of entertainment, finding it in such dubious places as the treatment room, where it was not unusual to find one peering over your shoulder and breathing down your neck while you were engrossed in a dressing. It was also customary to have to fight your way through a crowd of Watchers to resuscitate a collapsed patient. They were always the first on the scene, and the stickiest to remove.

Women were Watchers for women, and men for males, except in the children's wards. I was surprised at the number of men who came to stay with children: not only fathers, but uncles and older brothers as well. Contrary to the macho image I had of the Saudis, and especially the Bedu, they were often tender, gentle and concerned and took loving care of their charges. In the children's wards some of the mothers were a great help, but the men who came in to care for another male, grandpa for example, often sat about all day making a great mess, spitting on the floor, getting in the way, ringing the bell, using the phone, reporting the staff and being pests. Most of the complaints which filtered down to the director's office from the wards came from Watchers who had nothing better to do than find fault with matters of which they had no comprehension. Patients were mostly too busy or grateful for the nurses' attention to bother making complaints. Watchers were the bane of our lives.

Nonetheless, we had moments of fun. One day as I was passing through one of the children's wards I heard a terrific commotion: juvenile screaming, roars, bellows of outrage and terror. I met the company surgeon, a suave Indian, in the corridor. Laughing, he said to me, 'Do you want to know what all the noise is about? It is a boy being given a bath by his mother because it is his eighth birthday.'

I said, 'Well, I can understand he is shocked if he only gets a bath once a year on his birthday.' But the doctor shook his head. 'Oh, no, no. My goodness me, no. It is not because it is his birthday that he is getting a bath, but because it is his eighth birthday. It is not just a bath. It is The Bath, his first bath – since he was born!'

I found another novelty: VIP rooms.

These were not purpose built, but ordinary rooms which would have to be specially (and speedily) prepared when a VIP was heaving to on the horizon. I would be notified by the hospital director, then, as all rooms were four-bedded, I would have to hastily evict four patients and find places for them elsewhere – no mean feat at any time. Then, as if the genie of the lamp had conjured them up, masses of exotic Arabised Louis XIV furniture and a large expensive rug would appear, borne by a legion of Pakistani cleaners under the supervision of no less a personage than the hospital director himself. The unnecessary beds would be moved out, and the beautiful Persian carpet placed in the centre of the room, surrounded by three high-backed, throne-like chairs, heavily carved, gilded and upholstered in embroidered damask. To one side were richly ornate cabinets, side tables, and a highly decorative coffee table of onyx and gold plate. These items came up from the bowels of the basement and were whisked away immediately after the departure of the Exalted One.

Usually the VIP was a prince, another member of the royal family, or a person in some eminent position. (Most eminent positions were occupied by members of the royal family – solidarity they call it.) Said person would arrive with a servant or two of the same sex and often a relative in attendance. One I remember well was a prince from the ruling family of Medina who came in for a series of tests to investigate a possible heart condition. He stayed for only two days and was a charming man with impeccable manners who graciously said, 'minfadlik' and 'shukran', 'please' and 'thank you', before and after all his requests.

At the other end of the social scale, a Bedu walked into casualty one day and said he wanted something done about the pain in his side. On removing his cloak, it was discovered that he had the remains of a spear, at least a foot long, sticking out between his ribs. It had apparently been acquired in a tribal altercation with one of his brethren and he had borne it for two days, the time it took him to get to the hospital by camel. He recovered rapidly on antibiotics.

Just as bizarre was the case of a male patient, admitted for a hernia operation, who arrived smelling powerfully of Attar of Roses. After he had gone to the theatre for his operation the next morning, a large empty bottle that contained this extract was found under his locker. On his first postoperative day he went into full-blown DTs. When this was brought to my attention, he was perched on top of his bed-head fighting off all comers with his urinal. Having succeeded, he went galloping off down the corridor dragging behind him intravenous tubes, bottles and bandages (for all the world like a re-enactment of *The Curse of the Mummy*), with the staff in hot pursuit. All this activity was accompanied by the most fearful noise as he shrieked, '*Shaitan! Shaitan!* the devil!' Three bulky security guards, and large amounts of sedatives, eventually had their effect, but he continued to curse anyone who went near him, committing us all to Hell and the care of *Shaitan* for all time. I feared for his stitches and the results of his operation, as hernias should always be protected from exercise at first, but he appeared to emerge unscathed from the ordeal (which was more than some of the nurses did). After this episode I understood the implications of the huge numbers of 500ml bottles of very inexpensive perfume seen everywhere in the shops and supermarkets.

Traditional medicine is still practised, especially among the Bedu. This is administered by tribal medicine men and consists of herbs, spells, talismans and mutilations inflicted on the body in the belief that this will draw out the evil that is making the sufferer ill. Often a person is only brought to the hospital as a last resort after these methods have failed. Sometimes the patient dies because he has not received treatment in time and this reinforces mistrust of the hospital.

I saw several small children who had obviously been subjected to tribal medicine: they had multiple razor slashes, or rows of red weals made by hot coals from the cooking fire, or objects stuck under the skin. Sometimes children were removed from our care for several days and when they were returned there would be fresh welts, burns and cuts on their bodies.

In some areas, when twins are born, people believe that one of them is inhabited by a demon, so only one child will be reared. The surplus baby is left to waste away. This is also done in the case of an unwanted girl. Once newborn twins were admitted with their mother, and the staff noticed that one was failing to thrive. We suspected that the mother was not feeding this baby, so it was bottle fed by the nurses. This turned out to be a grave mistake as we were then left literally holding the baby, whose mother absconded one day with only the child she wanted. It was difficult to find a home for it, but in the end all was well as a kindly Sudanese on the staff added it into his already large family.

19 Riches and resuscitation

One day, the king came to stay in his castle on the mountain behind the hospital. This peak rose sharply out of a flat plain and reached a height of a thousand metres or more. Its top had been levelled to build an eagle's lair, a wonderful fortress with a commanding view, accessible only by a steep and heavily guarded road that went sharply up and wound around to the top. The king had a castle in every region of his kingdom and visited each for a few weeks of the year. He came to Medina always about this time, when the weather was at its best.

When the king was not in residence there were only a few lonely lights showing at night on the top of the mountain, but now from my window in the evenings I could see a great blaze of light. The castle was old but had been upgraded since the advent of the oil riches. I heard that there was a lift to the top and tunnels for hasty exits in case of attack. Terrorism was never far from the Saudis' minds and elaborate precautions were taken against it.

About once a year the king goes to the great mosque in Riyadh to pray for rain at Friday prayers, and it always rains afterwards, much to the delight and wonder of the populace. The grateful and admiring citizenry do not realise that the satellite tells the weatherman, who tells the king when to go down to the mosque.

The strangest aspect of the Saudi way of life, to a westerner, is the total segregation of males and females. There is absolutely no mixing socially, the sexes do not speak to each other or even look at each other, and married couples never touch or talk to each other when they go out. Men and women socialise separately, and not the way they do at the good old Aussie party, where the women sit inside and the men stand around the keg in the backyard.

All weddings are arranged. The bride's face is not seen by the groom until after the wedding, which must sometimes lead to some nasty shocks. A woman's dowry is paid by the groom to the bride's family, so that girls are not all that unwelcome as additions to a family, because a nice-looking little girl will eventually command a good bride price. Traditionally, it was camels, but much is changing with the oil money. I heard of one old man who became so enamored of one of the Filipino nurses at the hospital that he offered her ten pounds weight in gold bars, fifty camels and two flats in an apartment block. I think she was mad not to grab it. The preference in wives is for value for money; they like them chubby, plump or down-right fat. Once again, big is better: plump means well fed, and well fed means that you have enough of the good things of life.

It is unthinkable for a couple not to have children and a barren wife is divorced, or a second wife taken: women are still regarded by many as breeding stock and servants of men. Big families are still in vogue. It is a large, sparsely populated country, and the idea that lots of children is a sign of virility, as well as being an added strength to the tribe and family in old age, is still in style.

Only a short while ago over half of all children died owing to lack of medical facilities and infant welfare programmes. Male children are a status symbol as they are seen as proof of a man's potency. The rulers discourage birth control. They want more Saudis and more Muslims to strengthen their country. Doctors are told that they are not to prescribe contraceptives which, until 1980, were illegal, and are reported and punished if they do. Male babies are always circumcised, as part of the religious rites of Islam. Many of the laws and rules of Islam are very similar to Jewish ones, because the Jews have had a great influence on the peoples around them.

It is still possible by law to have four wives, but it is not so often now that men take more than two. The Koran clearly stipulates the conditions under which a man may have more than one wife: each wife must be treated equally and fairly. She must have a house the same as the others, and everything a man gives to one wife he must give to the others, whether it is material goods or love and affection. You would have to be wealthy to set up four separate households, and dealing with all your wives fairly and honestly could prove to be not only expensive but also exhausting, as you trotted from house to house like the local tomcat. There could also be a spot of trouble if they ever got together and compared notes. The very wealthy have large palaces in which each wife has her own quarters in a separate compound. This would save a bit of shoe leather.

Concubines are not restricted in number, but the enormous *harems* of the past are going out of fashion. They still exist, though there are fewer than before, because they are too expensive and it is now difficult to obtain large numbers of women for *harems*.

At the end of November the deputy chief nurse had still not been replaced and Len Fitch, my Illustrious Leader, wanted to go on leave before Christmas. He asked me if I would take on the deputy's job if the appointment was approved by MOH so that I could relieve him for his holidays. I accepted and was officially promoted to the position of deputy chief nurse. This was no mean feat. To get an appointment from MOH is tough once you're in the country, though any idiot can get one from outside. They are deeply suspicious of internal appointments of foreigners: possibly because of their own rife nepotism.

The higher up the ladder you went, the more hassles and problems you encountered, but it at least took your mind off the privations and isolation of the place. I thought that if I had a more interesting job I might even manage to stay there until the end of my contract. It was unlikely now that I would get a transfer out of Medina, so I decided, *Ensh'allah*, to finish my contract. With time off for good behaviour (or deducted for leave), I would have only seven and a half months of my sentence left to serve and could be off at the end of July.

I spent the next few days being orientated, then assumed command in the capacity of acting director of nursing. Early in December I found myself finally sitting in the boss's chair, asking myself if I was mad. What sane person, having seen first hand what it entailed, would have taken the job on voluntarily?

I had a good-sized office with a huge shiny desk and a Pakistani called Yusef to polish it every morning. But, by the end of the first day, I felt like hanging a sign on the door that said Complaints Department. The doctors came to complain about the nurses, the nurses complained about the doctors, the patients complained about them both and the visitors complained about absolutely everything. I think they had all been saving up until Len went away because he never listened to anyone. I managed to struggle through that first day with no catastrophe falling on my head, despite the Saudis' views that I was only a woman doing a man's job. By placing myself in this position I knew that I had left myself vulnerable. I accepted that I could be blamed and punished for anything that any of the five hundred and sixty nurses in my charge might do wrong, or on the whim of any crazy patient or doctor or other person who might complain to the hospital director.

One thing happened the next day which alleviated the situation somewhat. The hospital director, Mr Jamil, was sacked. Well, that's not what they called it, but the prince removed him elsewhere after someone of influence had complained about him. It was a relief. One of his favourite expressions, in his limited and fractured English, when referring to the nurses, was 'paralyse them'. He actually meant penalise them, but it was only slightly less malevolent, and who was brave enough to correct him?

I seemed to get along just fine with the new hospital director and he promised me all kinds of improvements for patient care. I withheld my enthusiasm for fear of disappointment, but continued to do Len's job for several weeks and some of the improvements were forthcoming.

The worst problem was the chronic shortage of nurses. We were about one hundred understaffed for a hospital of this size. There were huge outpatient and emergency clinics to staff, as well as the five hundred inpatient beds. To make matters worse, many nurses were used in non-nursing capacities in ancillary departments.

When I was not officiating in the complaints department, I did daily inspection rounds of the hospital, examining it from the basement to the fifth floor, which took about two hours. The director of nursing is responsible for everything to do with nursing, staffing, allocation of beds, and the day-to-day care of the patients, wards and departments. The directors of departments were all on an equal level, under the control of the chief administrator who was under the hospital director. Len was away for Christmas. Talk about Christmas Eve in the Workhouse. It was indeed the dreariest Christmas I have ever spent, but then it did not feel at all like Christmas: no decorations, no tree, no prezzies, no turkey, no holiday and, worst of all, no Christmas cheer. I wrote plaintively to my family requesting that they think of me over their Christmas goodies and most especially, the cheer! I received a few pretty Christmas cards from home, which I, greatly daring, stood on the table in my room.

There is a law against the practice of any religion except Islam in Saudi Arabia and it is a crime to profess any other faith, so it is illegal to celebrate Christmas. Though Saudi Muslims revere Christ as a prophet they strongly oppose the practice of Christianity. It is a grave offence to own a bible or a crucifix, even as a piece of jewellery on a chain around the neck. If you arrived in the country wearing one, it would be torn from your neck at customs.

After Christmas four of the Korean nurses were deported from the country. They had been heard singing Christmas carols in their room on Christmas Eve. The *matawain* had been on the lookout for such behaviour, and had been doing inspections of the quarters hoping to catch someone celebrating. What you did in your own room was not exempt from the law of the *matawain*. When we were at work they sometimes checked our flats looking for incriminating evidence of our decadence; rude pictures, dirty books, forbidden tapes or videos. Even the harmless old *Women's Weekly* could incur a hefty prison sentence, as it has the odd underwear advertisement.

When Len returned in late January I resumed as his deputy, having now the inside knowledge to continue along my own lines with plans for improving things, especially the lot of the nurses. Their morale was low, for as well as being overworked, the nurses generally felt that they got the blame for everything that went wrong. And they did. In the Arab world there must always be someone to take the blame for a mishap and that person must be punished. There seemed to be no logic about how that person was selected. Quite often it was merely the one in charge, or the lowest in the pecking order. Sometimes it was both and they were both punished.

As the deputy director of nursing I still listened to complaints, supposedly in Len's absence, but it seemed that he was never there when anyone came to complain. (Or was it that people waited for these times deliberately, as he was not so easy to complain to?) I also signed never-ending bits of paper, stood in for him when he was not around and continued to do daily inspections of the hospital because he did not. Operating from an office next to his which housed the nursing office staff and Sister Fatma, I started some badly needed programmes. The first floor was no longer mine and had been taken over by a new arrival, a young Dutch male nurse who seemed the most likely the company had produced yet.

For a start, there were no fire plans or drills for the

hospital. There were fire exits at each end of every floor, but the doors leading to them were for some unaccountable reason secured with a huge padlock and chain and no-one had any idea where the keys were. The hospital was a death trap. In the case of a fire it would have made the original Towering Inferno look like a blaze of one-candle power.

There was no safety officer employed, so I decided to take on the job unofficially. Some of the practices I uncovered were outrageous enough to make a real safety officer's hair stand on end. One of the cleaners on the ground floor, for example, had somehow been given the extra job of supplying a constant stream of tea to a couple of Saudis. For this operation he had been given a spirit burner and a good supply of fuel – methylated spirits – with which he heated the water for the tea in his broom cupboard. Imagine my astonishment when, on my inspection round, I opened the door to this cupboard and found it not only occupied, but also with a fire in it.

Now I believe the story that the Saudia plane that caught fire on the runway and exploded, killing everyone aboard, did so because a Bedu lit his spirit stove in the aisle to make his coffee while he was waiting for the plane to leave.

I started a lifting instruction programme for all the nursing staff because, whatever else they may have been taught in their nurse's training, lifting had not been included. They had not the slightest idea how to lift or move a patient without hurting them or themselves. The sick leave as a result of injured backs was prodigious. I also started a cardiac pulmonary resuscitation programme. A CPR team existed, but their performance was a sort of slapstick comedy. For a start, the telephonists, without English, made the call for CPR in Arabic and, as most of the nurses and some of the doctors had no Arabic, it was largely ignored. Eventually I convinced the hospital director to get them to make the call in English. Cardiac resuscitation was often applied to a patient who was merely fast asleep. The hapless victim woke from a peaceful slumber to find somebody, often an infidel, jumping up and down on his chest.

If ever you did arrive at the scene of a genuine cardiac arrest, it was to find either no-one at all, or the entire hospital assembled at the bedside, including the cleaners, kitchen staff, visitors and other patients, who insisted that it was their right to enjoy the drama. It didn't matter how many times they were asked to go. They would just sidle back. There were also outbreaks of professional jealousy between the doctors about who should help. In casualty once I saw two doctors, an Egyptian and an Indian, come to blows, slapping each other across the inert body of the luckless patient over which one of them was to insert the intravenous line.

In the nursing department I managed to improve the night duty stint by changing the hours to ten a night for five nights. This allowed the nursing staff to have two nights off afterwards, which was much better than only one sleep day. And I persuaded the MOH not to deduct meal times from the staff on nights and evenings, thus lessening the burden somewhat, because you always remained on call on these shifts even when you were in the dining-room. Now that I was working as the deputy I only worked during the day, so I did not reap the benefits, but I was told that it was a vast improvement. At least it made the nurses feel that there was someone on their side, and this was good for morale.

146

Instituting these plans and programmes required a lot of time sitting in various Saudi department directors' offices hoping to persuade them to support my plans. In time I came to realise that my intuition that Saudis treated some western women as honorary men was right. It was the only way they could deal with us. I was the first western woman that some of them had had contact with. We were generally thought of either as professional people, or as prostitutes; it all depended on the way you conducted yourself. If your approach was sexless and business-like, you were treated with respect, but foreign women were warned not to associate with Saudi men in illicit friendships in any way. The consequences could be disastrous.

I met most resistance to my new programmes from the nurses, and they were the ones I was most trying to help. Like all humans they were afraid of anything new. I had most difficulty convincing them that they must keep their working areas clean, directly or indirectly by instruction to the cleaning staff. They refused to see that it was their responsibility to provide a clean environment for their patients or that quality nursing care is not possible in a filthy setting, but against the odds I persevered and eventually there was a noticeable change.

20 Servitude and 'suicide'

A few weeks after Len's return from leave his contract finished and was not renewed by the company. He left the kingdom in a state of high dudgeon, furious because they did not want him any more.

It was only after Len's departure, while I was waiting for his replacement to arrive, that I learned from a hospital circular that I had been appointed to his position as chief nursing officer of the King Fahid Hospital. The translation of the circular read as follows:

Bismallah al Rachman al Raheem

'In the name of Allah, Most Merciful, Most Compassionate, Peace be upon you and the Mercy and Blessings of God. The Honourable Director of The King Fahid Hospital, Medina, announces today the appointment by the Ministry of Health, of Sister Lydia Laube as the most Excellent Director of Nursing.

'May Allah, The Beneficent, grant her all help and wisdom in her path. Signed, Abdullah Ibn Rashid Al Rachman.'

It was a great surprise. Although I was the logical person to take over, having been approved as the acting director and having shown that I could do the job, it was harder to be promoted through the ranks than to obtain a job from outside. Later I learned that senior people from the Ministry of Health had visited the hospital and checked on me and had told the head of the company that they intended to appoint me. It had not occurred to any of them to consult me. I saw the hospital director and told him that I would accept the post, and that I would stay until the end of my contract. So I took possession of the boss's chair and desk and resumed control of the Complaints Department. I was busy from morning until late at night and often long after hours.

About this time something happened which gave me a startling insight into one aspect of the Saudi way of thinking. One evening when I had been working late in my office, I took a walk through casualty and found a real commotion going on. The Filipino nurse in charge asked me to help with her problem. She told me that a Saudi woman had brought in her Filipino servant girl who claimed she could not walk. This was understandable; an X-ray showed that the girl had a badly broken ankle which needed setting under general anaesthetic. When the woman discovered that the girl would not be able to work, as she would have her leg in plaster for some time, she flatly refused to allow the operation. The doctor could not persuade her otherwise and was about to send the girl back home with her. Now if this was done, the girl would never walk again and what the Saudi woman would do with her was uncertain. She did not seem very charitable. I was horrified, and asked the doctor to reconsider. He said he could not operate without the consent of the girl's employer.

'Does this woman own her?' I asked.

And he replied, 'She is her employer. She does what she likes with her.'

I asked why the girl could not give consent for herself, as she was over twenty-one.

149

He looked at me as if I had taken leave of my senses.

I said again and louder, 'Does she own this girl?'

And he shouted back, 'Of course she does!'

This doctor was a Palestinian, but there were two other doctors involved, both Indian and obviously afraid to oppose him for fear of being reported. Because he was an Arab and they were not, his side would be taken by those in authority. A heated argument between the four of us ended when I said, 'Over my dead body does this girl leave here without a plaster.' Only when I took hold of the wheelchair and pushed the girl into the casualty theatre, declaring that I was going to plaster her leg myself, did they see that I was in earnest. They capitulated and did the operation. I feared that I only heard of this incident because the girl was a Filipino and so were the nurses in casualty. If she had been an Indian, for instance, I probably would not have been asked to help and she would have been abandoned to her fate.

The servants of the Saudis were often referred to as slaves, as were we, and this is not so hard to understand when you realise that slavery was only officially abolished in this country fifteen years ago. I heard that despite this, slavery still flourishes. The slave market may have gone, but it is by no means certain that the trade in mankind does not continue. Today, dark rumours persist of the buying and selling of human beings in the secretive centre of Arabia.

The Koran contains clear instructions about the treatment of female slaves and servants, but the new slaves do not come under these rules; they are not considered part of the Arab culture, where all women are under the protection of a man – husband, father or brother. There is a brother of the king, a certain prince, (and there are a great many of them, as the old king had forty-three sons and more than twenty daughters, and the royal family numbers over four thousand) who boasts that he has a woman in his *harem* to represent every country of the United Nations. His *harem* numbers several hundred and he maintains it in the style to which he has been accustomed. Every now and then he hires a jumbo jet and takes them all shopping to Paris or New York. He is getting old now, so his *harem* is mainly a matter of status. The women may be there by choice, but perhaps they're not: one does not resign from the *harem* on whim. They would not be allowed to leave without the prince's permission, so it is a type of slavery, although probably the latest European and non-Arab members come voluntarily. They have an incredibly opulent life and are retired usually at about thirty, and given a lump sum cash settlement or a pension. But no-one knows what happens to other girls in smaller *harems*.

The prince who owns the enormous harem was known to someone I worked with, a woman who had been a friend of the English nursing sister who ran the palace clinic. She told me about an old lady in the *harem* who had been captured in a slave raid in the Yemen when she was twelve. When she reached the age of sixty the present prince, who must have inherited her from his daddy, decided to let her go. She was given a little apartment at the back of the palace, but she was devastated at being removed from the *harem* and felt so lonely that she spent all her days at the clinic so that she would have someone to talk to. No life existed for her other than the life she knew in the *harem*.

Nothing has changed from the old days of raiding and taking slaves to do the manual work which is too demeaning for even the poorest Bedu, except that now the slaves are bought legally as contract workers, the new slave class. The Saudis have unwittingly committed themselves to a foreign labour force. The Riyadh airport, for example, needs ten thousand people to keep it running. Slaves are still treated much the same as before – some badly, some well, depending on the employer – but many of the Saudis seemed to confuse employing with possessing. Now, as then, the more useful and more valuable the slave, the better he or she is taken care of. In the hospital the staff with higher qualifications were treated much better than the cleaners, for example, and we were supposedly able to go home when our contracts expired, but this was not always the case. Hundreds of western workers were kept in the kingdom after their contracts were finished because their employers would not, or could not, get them exit visas. One person I knew about was a bio-dynamic technician, the only one of his kind, and when his contract was up, he was refused an exit visa until his replacement came. The company was slow to find a replacement, and the last I heard he was still there eight months later, working and waiting. Another was an English nursing supervisor who had signed for a theatre full of instruments and equipment in good faith, trusting fool that he was, and when it came time to get his clearance to leave, he discovered that most of it was missing and probably always had been. In order to leave he had to get someone else to sign for the equipment. The person taking over from him was an Arab, and wise to this game, he refused. So there the English supervisor sat, unemployed and unpaid for four months. The company did little to help but, in the end, with a lot of subterfuge and the aid of two Arab friends, he managed to escape. He somehow obtained a leave visa (easier to get than an exit visa) and slipped out of the country. The hospital director was furious when he discovered he had gone and heads would have rolled if he could have found out whose head to roll.

The position of the lower class of contract worker was much different from ours, or from those who worked for government departments, such as MOH. Some of them came to work for private people or small companies, being recruited by agencies in the surrounding Muslim countries and Pakistan, Afghanistan, The Sudan, India and the Philippines. Large numbers of these workers were brought in: there were between three and four million foreign workers in Saudi Arabia, mostly non-European. Ostensibly they were free to go when they wished and were supposed to be paid, but that was not always the case, and all passports were taken on arrival, as mine had been. Of all the contract workers at the hospital, and there were several companies contracted to provide different services, I did not see one worker who had been given the promised wages and conditions. Some were treated appallingly, and could not get out if the employer failed to pay them, or get them an exit visa. Some received only a fraction of the promised wages and were there for years, with no way of getting out. Some of the men got fed up with working twelve hours a day, seven days a week, with no food and no wages and gave up and ran away into the desert to join communes that had sprung up there. I suppose they lived off the charity of their fellow Muslims. At least they were better off than the countless girls employed as maids in private households. They were kept in *purdah*, rarely venturing out of the house, and they usually had no recourse to help of any kind if their employer treated them badly. One girl, a Filipino maid in a private house, was brought to the hospital, dead on arrival from loss of blood: she had committed suicide by cutting off her hands and feet; both hands and both feet. This is a traditional way of ridding yourself of an enemy, but what astounded me was that a doctor signed a death certificate giving the cause of death as suicide. He was told that it was so and he did not argue. Staff who had worked in other areas of Saudi said that they had seen instances of these 'suicides' of maid servants before and that it was not uncommon. They were always said to be suicides, no matter what the cause of death.

The story the nurses told me was that the girl had worked for years without being paid and finally demanded her money so that she could go home. She threatened to go to the Labour Court. This is a place in Medina which settles disputes, but you have to be Muslim to get to it for a start and then, if the employer hears of it, look what happens to you.

Another way of disposing of troublesome or unwanted people is to throw them off the roof or the balcony of the house, as in the much publicised case of an English nurse and a European man in Riyadh. It is commonly believed here that they were murdered, that the girl was raped and the man tried to come to her aid, but that those involved were of too high a rank to be accused without serious consequences. When the girl's father came to investigate the matter, he was treated with unfailing courtesy, politely interviewed and received endlessly until he gave up and went home.

Another Filipino maid was admitted to the hospital after she had 'fallen' from a roof-top (with a little help from her friends). She was also diagnosed as having attempted suicide, but she did not die, and while she was in intensive care someone from the household came and tried to smother her with a pillow. I put a guard by her bedside, but eventually she died.

Once an Indonesian maid was brought in with a cut throat and multiple stab wounds to her chest, back, arms, face and even the top of her head. She was placed in intensive care in a terrible state and very nearly died. Her diagnosis was also attempted suicide. The cut throat and some stab wounds she could have administered, but she would have to have been a double jointed contortionist to have stabbed herself in the middle of the back and the top of the head with such force. This poor girl eventually spoke to one of the nurses who understood Indonesian, and she said that the master of the house regularly made advances to her and that she tolerated it when it was only sex, but had objected when he demanded of her acts that she considered unnatural. When she resisted he had attacked her, and then the rest of the family came and joined in the attack.

Another attempt was made on her life while she was in the hospital. She had recovered enough to be in a room on her own, and there someone came to visit her, pulled the stitches from her throat wound and gouged it open again. She was rushed to theatre and resutured, and a guard put on her door until she could be transferred to a hospital in Riyadh.

At one time a young unmarried Saudi woman was admitted who had made a genuine suicide attempt. She drank a can of insecticide and she really meant to die. She was pregnant, and nothing worse could happen to a woman in Saudi Arabia: it meant that, by the laws of this land, she had committed adultery and her punishment was to be stoned to death in the public square. She did not die, and was subsequently taken away by the police.

I had read that women were stoned to death for adultery, but really did not believe it until I saw the public square in Jeddah where the executions take place (revoltingly named by westerners Chop Chop Square) and heard them announced every week on the television news. Every Friday, after the main prayers of the day, the condemned are taken out into the public square in front of the mosque, and there the sentence of beheading, stoning or flogging is carried out. Stoning can be a very fast or a very slow way to die, depending on who is there and what their aim is like.

A few years ago there was much publicity given to the death of a princess: the story of how the Saudi princess Mishail was executed for adultery. She fell in love with a young man to whom she was not married and, when it was proved that they had conspired to meet alone on several occasions, a charge of adultery was brought against them. The princess tried to escape the country disguised as a man but was recognised by the passport examiner at the airport. Ironically, presenting herself at the airport as a woman in *purdah* might have saved her, because a man cannot ask a woman in *purdah* to show him her face. She was returned to her family and she, and the man, were publicly executed in Jeddah by the side of the Queen's Building. He was beheaded with a sword by, it is believed, one of the princess's male relatives. It took five blows to sever his head – not the work of the professional public executioner – the princess was given the dispensation of being shot, six times in the head, rather than stoned.

I had several first-hand accounts of punishments and executions from other foreigners who had witnessed them. It is forbidden for anyone to leave the place of execution until the sentence has been carried out and, if a foreigner happened to be in the vicinity of the public square when a punishment was about to happen, he would be deliberately propelled to the front and obliged to stand there, held in place by the press of the crowd. The *matawain* wanted their justice to be seen and broadcast because it acted as a deterrent. They especially wanted us to know that, despite our wicked and degenerate lives at home, we could not corrupt their people with our bad example.

An English technician described a public execution he had witnessed: 'The square in front of the mosque was suddenly full of police armed with machine guns, who stationed themselves between the open space and the crowd which gathered. A black van drove into the centre of the square from which the condemned man was led blindfolded. A police officer read the death sentence, and the public executioner, an enormous black man wearing a black cloak and with a huge broad sword in an ornate gold scabbard, stepped forward. The condemned man was pushed to his knees and his head positioned down. There was a breathless silence. The executioner unsheathed his sword, flourished it over-head and with one colossal blow slashed off the man's head. Streams of blood spurted everywhere and the head bounced on the ground. The crowd cheered. The police threw the remains into the back of the van and drove away.'

Saudi justice is based on a combination of the teach-ings of the prophet and tribal law. In some areas tribal law prevails: the male head of a family is still able to put to death a female who shames the family honour with a sexual sin: and the victim's family decides whether a murderer is executed or pays compensation and they may perform the execution themselves, in which case close male family members can all take a hand.

Punishment can be barbarous. The hundreds of Iranians and other troublemakers arrested at the time of the riots in Mecca were said to have been taken out over the Empty Quarter in a plane and sent sky-diving without the benefit of parachutes.

I was nervous when I heard stories like these. The power the Saudis had over you was so absolute, and the outside world was so shut-off, so remote.

21 The lowest ebb

I had always been aware that Islamic rules were strictly enforced at Medina because of its holy status, but recently a clampdown had begun. Things were getting decidedly worse for foreigners. There was a steady tightening of the religious law enforcement, as though the authorities feared that internal laxity might encourage attacks from outside. Saudi Arabia was especially fearful of Iran and its escalating war with Iraq. When I was still deciding whether or not to work in Saudi Arabia, I expressed my concern about this to the recruiters and was told that there was no cause for alarm. They said that Iran respected Saudi Arabia as the place of the holy sites and would never do it any harm. I no longer believed these platitudes. Iran has many fanatics who say that Saudi Arabia is not fit to be the keeper of the holy places and want to govern them themselves. They believe theirs is the only way and are itching to get in and straighten out the religion, not caring who or what they demolish. As they believe it would be *Al Jehad*, a holy war, and to fight to the death in a holy war is a sure and immediate ticket to heaven, this makes them very dangerous. They had already tried several times to land on the Saudi Arabian coast north of Damman, but had been repulsed. They attacked Kuwait, Saudi Arabia's next door neighbour, and it was said that Saudi Arabia would be next.

After the attacks on Kuwait began, President Reagan promised Saudi Arabia missiles for protection. I made up my mind then that I would not be travelling out through Singapore again. I had heard of the heat seeking missiles that Iran was firing at planes over the Gulf. The Iranians were reported to have said that they wanted to bring down a Saudi plane. Even if they were not trying they were probably such rotten shots that they could easily get one by mistake and, if not, the Saudis would.

Locally things were becoming worrying. Two English male staff from the hospital up the road were imprisoned for several days. They had climbed a hill behind the hospital to take some photographs of the countryside and were promptly arrested, possibly dobbed in by one of the legion of spies and informers employed at the hospital (as in any government place). They were finally released, but without their cameras, which are still doing time: Saudis have no concept of the tourist's insatiable urge to photograph everything. (Islam prohibits the depiction of anything, living or dead, so, in theory, all photography is forbidden.)

At KFH a couple of Filipino nurses, who were finishing their contracts and leaving the next day, decided to go out at three in the morning – they were on night duty and it was their supper time – to photograph the front of the hospital as a souvenir. Within seconds a policeman popped up out of the bushes and arrested them. Their cameras were confiscated but, fortunately, they had their exit visas and left the country that morning by the early plane before the police came back for them.

Then came the worst incident. It left me profoundly

shocked and determined to have done with the place as soon as possible.

One morning a messenger came to my office with a circular from the hospital director ordering me and all my staff to present ourselves in front of the recreation centre immediately after the mid-morning prayer. I signed the circular in assent and asked around, but no-one knew the reason for the meeting.

At the appointed time I fronted with the two Egyptian women from the office and found a large crowd assembling; all the nursing staff who could be spared or were off duty, domestics, cleaners, office staff and all the Saudi workers. Buses were arriving, bringing nurses from inside Medina, other hospitals in the area and the various clinics around the district. There was a large open area, traversed by a covered walkway, between the recreation centre and the shop, which was now rapidly filling with people. Men were on one side and women, all the Muslims veiled, on the other. It was intensely hot, so I waited in the shade of the walkway. I was completely at a loss, but began to feel apprehensive.

Then the *matawain* arrived, and I knew something unpleasant was going to happen. There was a commotion in the area of the shop and I saw several men pushing and pulling the Filipino tailor and his assistant out to a space cleared in the middle of the crowd. By now I was afraid but still quite unprepared for what was to come. Then I saw a Filipino nurse, who had been standing with a group of other women, suddenly seized by two *matawain* and also dragged to the centre of the cleared space in the enormous crowd, which formed a big circle around the victims. This cannot be happening, I thought. I began to feel unreal, as if I was in someone else's body looking down on this scene. The boys were pale and trembling. The girl was terrified and crying. The *matawain* produced a long, thin, bamboo stick. I went cold with terror as I realised that they were going to be whipped. I had to watch, although I didn't think I could bear it. The two Arab sisters held my hands and supported me and entreated me not to do anything, as I think they realised that I was about to interfere. 'You cannot interfere with the justice of the *matawain*. It is a grave offence,' they said.

By now the terrified nurse was almost hysterical. She was shrieking, weeping and saying, 'No! No!' The *matawain* held her firmly by the wrists with her arms extended. The third one with the whip intoned the list of her crimes, a reading from the Koran and an exhortation to Allah. On finishing, he raised his arm; the whip bent, and then cracked down on her back and legs. She screamed and would have fallen if she had not been firmly held. Worse still, the Saudi and Egyptian men at the front applauded and cheered. The two Filipino boys, who were held in front of the girl, watched appalled and petrified with fear. The girl was given fifty lashes. I fought back waves of nausea. She appeared to be unconscious at the end and was carried away and admitted to the hospital for treatment of her wounds and shock. The two young tailors received seventy lashes each and were then taken immediately to prison. Through it all we had to stand there. It was meant to convince us that we should not sin. Except for some of the Arab men, who enjoyed seeing God's wrath inflicted on the sinners, we were all punished. I hurt from that experience to this day. I had never before seen physical violence inflicted upon anyone. I abhor cruelty and have always refused to watch it, even on film.

Later the girl was deported, which was lucky for her,

except that she had lost her job and probably would not get another. The tailors were imprisoned for six months, with a flogging repeated every Friday, in the traditional manner after prayers. All their possessions were confiscated and they lost their livelihood. These people had no chance to deny or admit their crimes, as they had no warning that they were even accused. They did not know that they had already been tried and sentenced, until the sentence was about to be carried out. The crime was that the nurse had been seen to hand the tailor a video film: the assistant had done nothing except be present. It was customary to exchange films among the staff, but this instance had been witnessed by someone who saw any contact between male and female as unlawful, as indeed it is. It was said that the bland American film had forbidden sex scenes on it. That was highly unlikely. Maybe it had a couple of kisses, but that would be enough to give the *matawain* apoplexy. When it is understood that a father kissing his daughter on the cheek is cut from any film, you begin to comprehend how the authorities would view a kiss between lovers.

22 Escape to Egypt

In January I had been in Medina for four months and was entitled to ten days' leave. Some companies give leave after three months and even pay the fares, but not so Omega the Mean. Eventually leave was granted me for the middle of February. It was too far to go home for such a short time, so I decided to go to Egypt, which I had long wanted to see. As a child I had discovered the Egyptian room in the Adelaide Museum and I had been immediately enthralled. The mystery and wonder of it never left me.

But to leave, even for such a short time, it was necessary to get a hospital clearance. This involved visiting the head of every department to obtain his signature (they were all male – I was the first and only female head of a department ever seen at KFH) to say that I possessed nothing belonging to his department. I was lucky. I'd had the great good sense, after signing for my flat's furniture, which never did cause a problem, to steadfastly refuse to sign for anything else. So everyone signed my paper and I had my exit visa and my passport in my hand, but not until I arrived at the airport and my departure was imminent.

I had arranged my flight to Egypt through the company secretary, Ibrihim, who was Muslim and who went into Medina to buy a ticket for me. I was going directly from Medina to Cairo. It is the only direct international flight out of the country, apart from the capital and Jeddah, and mainly exists to cater for the pilgrims who come that way. The direct link with Cairo takes only an hour, crossing the Red Sea in an almost straight line. Two companies make this flight, Saudia and Egyptair, both on the same day at the same time. I chose to fly Saudia, as it had a much better record in the air safety stakes.

Setting about getting ready for my leave, I organised a temporary replacement; the deputy chief nurse, a Welshwoman of advancing years and generous girth whom the company had recently sent out. I got all my vaccinations up to date and stocked my first-aid kit. I made sure all my working parts were in good order, starting with a service and tune up on my teeth. I hoped I was about to see quite a bit of action in the eating department. The visit to the dentist did not get off to an auspicious start. I was given a card that announced that I would be seen by a Dr Killy. Sitting in the corridor awaiting his ministrations, I had for a companion in anxiety a sombre-looking Bedu who devoutly told the beads of his rosary all the while he waited. (Did he know something I did not?) But the dentist was only Maurice Kelly, a jolly, elderly Irishman who worked for the company, and who was, despite looking like Pig Pen, the gentlest, sweetest soul. He was the untidiest person you could ever meet, with a light dusting of cigarette ash all over him and his coat showing the vestiges of many of his recent meals. He was, before Saudi, a pædodontist, a specialist children's dentist. He spoke to me as though I was all of three years old, patted me on the head when he had finished, and said I was a good girl, and miracle of miracles, he did not hurt a bit.

On the day of my departure the company was obliged to take me to the airport and see me on the plane. They did not care what happened to me once I was aboard, for their responsibility for me was relinquished as soon as I was on my way out of the country. I was very apprehensive about going through immigration again, but the company representatives, who were Arab, assured me that my papers were in order and there would be no problems going out.

The plane left at half past two, but I had been told that I must be at the airport two hours beforehand. I thought this was excessive for such a small flight, but it took me every single minute of that two hours to get on the plane. It was a gruelling experience.

I had thought Medina airport to be just a sleepy little out-of-town place, but that was before I saw it on a pilgrim's day. *Umra* – a sort of mini pilgrimage – was just finishing and the pilgrims were going home.

I had also been told that boarding Saudia would not be like boarding Egyptair, who did not issue seat numbers to passengers. On the word 'go!' everyone surged forward and leaped for a seat, rather like playing musical chairs. Unfortunately, on this occasion, Saudia's plane was also full of Egyptians and, seat number or not, it is not the Egyptian way to stand in line in an orderly fashion.

When I arrived at the airport I saw a huge mountain of luggage outside the entrance doors and an ominously large crowd of people, pushing and shoving and doing their utmost to get in the door at the same time. The company reps took one look at this lot and abandoned me in the boiling sun at the back of the throng. I realised that if I wanted to get inside, I had to get in among the crowd and push and fight. A queue would have solved the problem in half the time, but no-one here had ever heard of one. In the end, I inserted myself in their midst, stood there, and was carried along like a leaf in the wind.

I have never seen anything like the gigantic pile of luggage that was going to travel on two small planes, most I hoped with Egyptair. In the crowd there were several Egyptian doctors from the hospital who were going on leave. They had the biggest suitcases I have ever seen (no doubt containing some of the missing toilet seats and other sundries from the housing) and several enormous bundles quite blatantly sewn up in hospital sheets.

Inside it was even worse. The reception area was packed solid with people and luggage. There seemed to be a separate counter for the pilgrims. I noticed that the people in white all surged towards one area, which had a lot more staff to speed things up; we Philistines surged to another. Eventually, after an hour or more of this claustrophobic bodily contact, I reached the counter. I had taken great care not to pack more than the twenty kilograms allowed, but no-one was charged for excess baggage, no matter how massive their luggage. Heaven help the overloaded plane at takeoff. Then I was propelled, under Other Person Power, to the entrance of the departure lounge. I was refused entry until I had retreated to immigration, where I had another struggle. The immigration official looked at my passport for what seemed ages and then took it away for someone in the office to examine. I began to feel afraid. My exit visa was being checked to see if I was permitted to leave the country. This seemed to take forever, and I now started to feel guilty as well. The official came back and asked me the obligatory, 'Where is your husband?' and when I settled that matter, he said, 'Why are you going out when you have only been here five months?'

'That's when I get my leave.'

'You don't get leave until twelve months.' He seemed very knowledgeable.

I replied that as I was not working for the Ministry of Health but a British company, I was different. He could see this, so he let me through the gate.

Finally I arrived in Egypt, the traumas of the airport forgotten. I had a wonderful holiday: I found the people to be warm and fun-loving and, although Muslim, not as severely repressed as the Saudi Arabians. They love to sing and dance and even have a drink or two. I had been longing for my leave so that I could see again a long, tall, cold, frosted glass of something wickedly alcoholic, mainly because it had been forcibly withheld from me. (I know now that in the days of prohibition I would have been making bath tub gin just for the devilment of it.) So the first thing I did was to install myself in the Long Bar of Sheaperds Hotel, another colonial institution, and order a gin and soda. Previously I had always mixed something with gin to disguise the taste. Now I wanted to know that it was there, to reassure myself that it was not fake booze, like 'Saudi Champagne'.

I explored Cairo from the hotel, took a five-day trip down the Nile by boat, visited Luxor (ancient Thebes), and Aswan and the mausoleum of the Agha Khan. I also went to Alexandria where I found my uncle's grave in the Commonwealth War Cemetery of Chatsby. He was the first Australian soldier to die in Egypt in World War II. I extended my holidays to three weeks by the expedient of sending a cable to say I was unavoidably detained. I had been told that this was an acceptable way to extend leave; a typical example of Arab deviancy (or diplomacy). There were those back at KFH who thought I would do a bunk and were quite surprised when I returned. Bunking is common, as it is far easier to get permission for holiday leave than to leave the country if your contract is not finished.

It was strange how freedom now affected me. I had, unbeknown and unnoticed, become accustomed to my deprived and constricted life. In the first few days of holidays I kept catching myself thinking how weird it was to be walking on the street with my head uncovered. It was as if the other was the real life and this the dream. It was frightening to contemplate later, when the strangeness wore off, that it had only taken a few months to reduce me to this. For a while it was very stressful trying to adjust. Other women told me they had the same experience.

At the end of three weeks, however, I was back to normal, and the thought of returning to that other life depressed me utterly. If I had not given my word (and left behind most of my belongings), I might have stayed in Egypt. It would have been easy to remain there and get a job in one of the international hospitals, where I could have had a much easier time and an interesting social life.

Reluctantly I took myself back to Medina, where I was collected at the airport by Roger and his deputy, who were delighted to see me. They deposited me at my flat, and I was once more back in *purdah* behind the *harem* walls.

23 Back in custody

We had no outings on our days off after I got back, for while I was away Mustafa ran into a donkey at high speed head on, coming back late at night from Yanbu. The company did not see fit to replace the bus so we waited for the repair of the old one. The donkey (RIP) was being claimed for by his owner, so the bus was not only beaten up, but also impounded by the police, as Mustafa had been for a few days, until the dispute was settled. The unfortunate Paul, the administrator's deputy, had been seated in the front, and was almost killed. He had severely damaged his knees where he connected with the windscreen. Mustafa was supposedly sacked, but so far had refused to understand anyone who told him to go. The hospital director said that he had to see Mustafa's relative who had obtained the job for him, and to whom matters must first be explained. At the time I left the kingdom, Mustafa could still be found sitting about in the company office at odd times of the day, and fronting regularly to collect his pay, even though another driver had been employed. The company were still waiting for the hospital director to see Mustafa's relative.

Towards the middle of March or *Shaban*, the weather was warming up quickly and it was back to sleeping and living with the airconditioner. The bus was still not available so I persuaded Roger to let a driver take several company women to the village *souk* in the company car. We did this a few times and it was on one of these occasions that I was arrested by both the police and the *matawain*.

Four of us – the Irish radiographer, the Indian doctor, the Scottish nurse, and I – were shopping when the call to prayer came on. Usually we would have gone to the bus, which used to stand in the street waiting for us, but the driver had taken the car and gone off on a mission of his own. We were standing on the step of a small cafe run by a Turk, and as he departed for his prayers he invited us to sit inside and wait. No-one locks up to go to prayers. He turned off the lights and we sat down around a table in the darkened room. It was hot and we were glad of his kindness. At any other time we would not have ventured inside a place like this, as they were for men only and it was quite unthinkable for women to enter one. As we sat there minding our own business, we saw a police prowl car, its distinctive black and white colour unmistakable, pull up outside. Two policemen jumped out, and running to the door of our cafe, began loudly pounding and banging on it, while shining a bright torch beam on us. Thinking it had nothing to do with us, we did as Saudi women would do and waited for some man to deal with it. The police then tried the door, found it open, came inside and launched into a stream of Arabic. I still thought it had nothing to do with us, but I attempted to answer with all the fluency I could muster with my ten words of Arabic. On the side I told the others to say nothing and sit still. By now I realised that we were the ones in trouble and I was thoroughly alarmed. After a while they gave up their questioning and one of them went to the patrol car, leaving the other to guard us. The former used the two-way radio in the car, and within minutes another prowl car roared up. You would have thought we were armed and deadly dangerous. Then another car arrived and from this emerged two *matawain*, the dreaded religious police. My anxiety sky-rocketed. These were the boys to really worry about. They began to interrogate us. We sat still with eyes cast down and waited for someone to claim us. Where was our driver?

The cafe owner and his two assistants came back from prayers. One of them, who spoke a little English, came over and told us that we had been arrested for being in the cafe at prayer time. The police demanded our papers. We produced a photocopy of passports, work permits, residency papers and visas, and a permit signed by the hospital director to allow us to be outside the compound on this night.

More interrogations followed. They seemed to be asking us if we had had anything to eat or drink which was unacceptable at prayer time. We had each taken a Pepsi out of the fridge, intending to pay the proprietor on his return, but we consistently denied this, trying to avoid trouble for him. Another police car arrived and shortly after, another. There were now countless police around us, as well as the two *matawain*.

I got up to test the water and moved towards the door. A policeman stepped up and firmly barred the way. There was no doubt about it. We were detained. I resumed my seat, quite terrified. They had obviously radioed to a higher authority, for next a chap in civilian dress and looking most important arrived in a big black car.

Just at this moment our driver, praise be to Allah, Most Merciful, chose to saunter along in search of us.

We were most fortunate that on this night we had as our driver Ibriham, otherwise known as Silver Tongue, a Sudanese of considerable charm. The Arabs love a good talker, and I am sure that it was only his skill of persuasion that saved us from prison.

The police arrested the cafe proprietor and his two assistants and took them to prison: they were men and should have known better. This was another of the times when being female was an advantage.

Ibrahim was allowed to drive us to the hospital and then was taken to the police station where he spent several hours explaining what he was doing driving women about at night. He said that we were merely ignorant and meant no harm. It would have been easier to explain if we had been in the company bus, which had Omega, King Fahid Hospital written on its sides.

At half past eleven, when I had just gone to bed, the phone rang. It was Sister Narcissus, who was a sort of house-mother to the nurses, a Filipino of liberal proportions, with a hypertensive personality and a great gift of the gab. 'The police are here and they are looking for some women who were out walking the streets unescorted. Whoever could that be?' she asked in an incredulous voice. When I told her it was me, she almost fell off her perch.

I think the police only came to check on us. Even though they had seen our papers they probably still did not believe we were allowed to be out. I heard no more so I can only presume that they wilted under the barrage they would have received from Sister Narcissus, who intimidated even the Saudis. She was one of the few Filipinos who had no fear of them. This loquacious lady was a Muslim, had been in the country for years, spoke fluent Arabic and, I think, had friends in the glorified upper regions of the MOH. A very formidable package was our Sister N, who could be a valuable ally or a bad enemy, and I therefore made a very special effort to bring her under the spell of my charm.

Three days later Ibrahim told me that the poor men from the cafe were still in prison, but I believe they were released after a few more days. I was distressed that we had been the reason for their plight, but nothing could be done to help them.

About this time Roger, our ineffectual administrator, completed his contract and moved on. His position was filled by his efficient deputy. No-one mourned his passing.

24 Spitting images

Ramadan, the ninth *Hegira* month and the month of fasting, was upon us. It starts with the first official sighting of the new moon by a reliable witness, usually one of the *Imams* from Mecca. For the entire month Muslims must abstain from eating, drinking, smoking and copulation from sunrise to sunset, from about five in the morning, just before the dawn prayer, until about nine at night, after the last prayers for the day. At the end of the month when the moon has reached its final phase, the holy man states again that the moon is right and *Ramadan* ends with the ten day feast of *Idl Fittr*.

Fasting time begins when, in the words of the Koran, a black thread can be differentiated from a white one: dawn is just breaking and the *Fadja*, or dawn prayer call, is about to sound. It is forbidden for a Muslim to break the fast, a crime punishable by law. A non-Muslim must not eat, drink or smoke in front of a Muslim or anywhere in public, and any infringements are dealt with severely.

The fast is taken so seriously by some Muslims that they will not even swallow their saliva. Spitting is the unofficial national sport of Saudi Arabia. Patients and visitors spit on the floor in the hospital or anywhere else they fancy, but its incidence increased dramatically in *Ramadan* until it became a veritable epidemic. Now the nursing staff and cleaners started doing it, and several times I found a male nurse spitting in a sink, bin or hand basin on the wards.

As non-Muslims we were not expected to keep the fast, but the rules of not eating or drinking in front of a Muslim made life difficult and deprived us as well. In a way we unbelievers joined the fast – for a start the dining-room was closed for the duration of *Ramadan*. Although company staff were not officially permitted tea breaks, we usually managed to have cups of tea or coffee during the day. It did not seem to upset anyone if those who had their own offices had a cup of something on their desk. There was a small immersion heater available in the *souk* which, when applied to a cup of water, quickly produced a hot beverage. Company staff carried these in their pockets and called to see a colleague with an office when the need arose. Now, when even sneaking a quick sip of water necessitated slipping behind a closed door, a cup of tea was out of the question. As the only woman with an office, I had to maintain decorum, and all my dealings had to be in full view of people in the corridor.

During *Ramadan* working hours were reduced and prayer times extended. Saudis now only worked five hours a day and the MOH, as a special dispensation, worked eight hours for a five-day week. Some of the company staff were Muslim and, as fellow brethren, were entitled to some recognition of their fasting. The only way they could be given reduced hours was to give them to us all, so *Ramadan* was a welcome respite. It was wonderful to have two whole days off duty every week. I would not have believed how hard it was to work fifty hours a week.

The shops were shut all day until after dark during *Ramadan*. We went to the village a couple of times, but we did not go to Jeddah or Yanbu. All the restaurants were shut.

Television, already limited, became even more so. Religious programmes replaced *Sesame Street* and other popular frivolities. The nightly prayers in the mosque at Mecca or Medina were broadcast in full. Evening prayers went on until after eleven most nights and were broadcast over the loud speaker from the compound mosque. I had to wear earplugs if I wanted to go to sleep. Although it was forbidden for a non-believer to enter a mosque or the holy cities, it did not seem to bother anyone that we could watch it on television. Lengthy sermons preached by the Imams were given English subtitles for the benefit of those Muslims who did not speak Arabic: some knew only the traditional words of greeting and the prayers, although it behoved them to try to learn it.

I had read of the early visitors who had come to the country in attempts to explore and investigate this secretive place. Even up to the the 1920s it was perilous to travel through the country; it was certain death for non-Muslims. Arabs in this part of the peninsula had a distrust of foreigners that bordered on xenophobia. After the unification of the separate warring tribes and sheikdoms by the first king of Saudi Arabia, early this century, some non-Muslim travellers were allowed to go through, but they were still far from safe to journey freely. Later, when the need for foreign workers arose, King Abdul Aziz said that foreigners were a threat to his country's religion, morals and stability and that workers should be kept at a distance and sent home as soon as the work was done. The law of death to the infidel whose presence defiled the holy cities of Mecca and Medina still held. I could not discover if the penalty would still be death, but there is nothing to say otherwise. Naturally, this rule of exclusion excites the imagination of some people, and I had a first-hand account by someone who, on pain of death, had unlawfully visited Medina. Luckily for this foolhardy woman, the laws of *purdah* worked in her favour, but it was a crazy act.

Once a month the Muslim nurses living in the King Fahid hospital compound were taken by an MOH bus into Medina on a Friday to the Great Mosque of the Prophet for the holy day prayers around midday. Everyone went in full *purdah*, so this woman only had to find two or three Filipino nurses to go with. I had thought this would be difficult, but the Filipino Muslim faith is nothing like the fanatical Arab faith and they seemed to regard this as a great joke. All the non-Muslim had to do was to keep quiet and tag along; her presence would be explained to any who asked as a new staff member from India who spoke only English and her own dialect and was very shy. The visit went uneventfully, with a brief visit to the mosque and a quick trip to the market before arriving back at the place where the bus would return to collect them. The description of mysterious Medina was disappointing. She said it was uninspiring, dirty and rather like any other Saudi provincial town.

In the hospital the fasting was not doing the Muslims any good, especially the nurses. Everyone got a little light-headed after a while and began behaving rather oddly. The locals were all pranging their cars, and the nurses fell asleep on the job. Thank goodness more than three-quarters of them were non-Muslim and not fasting. I suspect that one or two Muslims might have sneaked a little sip of something now and then, but most were pious and took it very seriously, so that by half-way through the month they were beginning to show signs of wear. One of the reasons for the universal sleepiness was that, during *Ramadan*, night and day were reversed: because they could not eat during the day, they stayed up most of the night eating to catch up. This was all very well if you had only a few camels to watch, but came unstuck when you were supposed to be working in a hospital.

The mail service, never brilliant, went right off as the postal pixies did not bother to sort or deliver the mail. Consequently, very few letters arrived at the hospital, a privation for the expatriates whose main source of comfort was their mail from home.

At last the holy man in Mecca proclaimed that the moon was in its right phase, and the end of *Ramadan* was announced. Now was the time for the festival of *Idl Fittr*. I was informed of this late at night by a phone call from the hospital director. He also told me that it was my duty to go with him to the hospital first thing in the morning to play gracious hosts, dishing out flowers and good wishes to the patients. The following day was Friday and my day off but, regrettably, I had to rise at the usual time for work. It was not unusual to be summoned to work on my day off. So, I presented myself at the director's office and we began a tour of the entire hospital. It was like a royal progress. The director swept along in front in his new white *thobe* (everyone gets new clothes to celebrate this festival) with me in tow, two steps behind. The rearguard was made up of a couple of his male secretaries, also looking brand new, the administrator, and several male helpers to carry the flowers. I felt like Lady Bountiful dispensing largesse to the peasants, but I think they only took me along to show me off as their token woman.

We swept regally into the first room which was on a male ward. The director wished the foremost patient a blessing in Arabic and I stepped up and gave him a single carnation and said, 'Id Marburak', the equivalent of Merry Christmas or some such. The patient looked thunderstruck and burst into tears. Not a fortunate beginning. But it did get better.

Word of our doings must have spread before us because, as we progressed, the general idea seemed to have sunk in and some even said, 'Shukran', thank you, and returned the blessings. When we got to the female wards the women were a lot more receptive and some handled the visit with aplomb, and were thrilled with their carnations. Flowers were a rarity and regarded highly. They were also extremely expensive, being flown in from some country to the north. Each person was rationed to one flower, but they were prettily wrapped in a piece of cellophane and tied with a ribbon.

The women had been warned there were men coming and were all covered in *abeyas* and veils. Many took my hand and kissed it. Others shook my hand or embraced and kissed me on both cheeks depending on whether they already knew me or not.

One small Sudanese girl, wearing for the festival her new dress, which was covered in bows and ribbons, took my hand and, smiling up at me, accompanied me the rest of the way around the hospital. There were many children visiting the hospital and they all had new clothes for this special day, the little boys so hand-somely dark in their sparkling white new *thobes* and bright red-checked *guteras*, the little girls in those wonderful ornate long dresses.

The women were very happy to have someone to whom they felt they could talk, even if it was only through an interpreter. They would never have spoken to Len Fitch. It would not have been fitting.

I found the women soft and gentle and very charming. The Beduin women made up the larger proportion of those I saw, although most of the town Arab women were sweet too. They were unsophisticated in a shy and pleasant way, and once they got over feeling in awe of me, were very interested to know about me. I never noticed before, but at home no-one except your family is ever interested in your feelings the way Arab women were. They would ask me if I was happy, was I lonely without a husband, did I miss my family, and countless other questions. They really cared to know: it was not just idle chat. The women, once they got over their initial terror, kissed and touched me a lot, as they do each other. As I went around the hospital, patients and Muslim female staff would kiss me on both cheeks or the hands in greeting and frequently took my hand and held it when talking to me. I do not like strangers kissing or touching me, but their actions did not offend me. I found it consoling when I was having a bad day.

Men show affection for each other in the same way. The hospital director arriving for work in the morning could be seen progressing down the hospital corridor, robe flapping behind him, being kissed noisily by his male associates or, at prayer time, going off to the mosque hand in hand with a friend.

Having done our bit to celebrate *Idl Fittr* in the hospital, the Saudis went away for a big feast, but all I got out of it was to lose half my precious day off. After *Ramadan* there were ten days of the *Idl Fittr* festival. The Saudis had these as holidays, but we heathens did not.

I wondered sometimes about the joys permitted to the faithful. I was told it was written that the earthly pleasures allowed to men were prayer, work, women and perfume. No mention was made of the worldly delights allowed for women. Perfume would be the only item that would interest me out of that list.

With the end of *Ramadan* came the re-opening of the dining-room and kitchen, and we could now once again eat openly. The dining-room was a huge, hall-like affair, with a long counter at one end. Behind it stood a line of male servers, mostly Indian or Pakistani, dressed in white jackets, trousers, aprons and cooks' hats. (A nice piece of psychology was used there, thinking maybe that we would be confused into believing someone in this den of iniquity really did know how to cook.) The servers were in charge of enormous metal cauldrons and stainless steel dishes which contained some unappetising matter. We passed by in line and they slapped food onto our plates, much as they do in the army. There was a floor-to-ceiling curtain running the entire length of the room that effectively cut it in two. One side was for females and the other for men. This was necessary, as Sister Fatma explained to me, for an Arab woman could not lift her veil to eat in the presence of a man, even if it were not forbidden for the sexes to mix. Even married couples who both worked at the hospital were forbidden to eat together.

Some of the hospital staff were veiled. There were Arab Muslim women, wives or family of doctors or other staff from neighbouring Arab countries who worked as technicians and at other ancillary jobs, and were in *purdah*, although they wore veils with eye slits leaving their eyes uncovered. Sometimes the veils were white to match their uniforms. These Arab girls' families were considered very permissive for allowing them to work at all but would have insisted on their retaining their veils in the hospital.

Not that I would have wanted to watch the men eat. Most of them ate in the Arab manner, with their hands only. Mind you, I often did too, out of pure necessity, as the sole cutlery supplied was plastic and no match for the tough old chicken we got every day. (We would have stolen any decent cutlery as there was nothing to eat with in the housing.)

The food was edible and possibly nourishing, but it was boring beyond belief. It was devoid of taste and its presentation was horrible. I ate it gladly after the first few days when I very nearly starved to death because I had no idea where or how to get anything. Although MOH staff had all meals provided free, company staff had to pay eight riyals for a meal. And we were only allowed to eat in the dining room when we were on duty.

After I got myself organised, I had lunch in the dining-room and otherwise existed on fruit, cheese and a kind of muesli I made from ingredients I found in the *souk*: tinned Quakers' oats, imported from England and for which the locals obviously had an affection, sesame seeds, raisins and peanuts, bought in bulk from large hessian bags. I got fresh fruit from the *souk* and tinned fruit from the compound shop. As I was not able to ask for what I wanted, it took time rummaging and poking around in bags on the floor and among heaps of dusty goods on rickety shelves, to find what I wanted.

There was a good supply of tinned and bottled fruit juice in the shop and several brands of pseudo wine: grape juice disguised in green bottles with proper wine labels, corks and all. There was non-alcoholic beer that looked and tasted like the real thing, so the chaps said. I would not waste my time trying it. The grape wine tasted exactly like grape juice pretending to be wine. But I like grape juice, fermented or otherwise, so I continued to buy it. At the hotels we visited I enjoyed the 'cocktails' from the extensive lists, but they did not delude me for a minute. The famous 'Saudi Champagne' – Perrier water mixed with apple juice – tastes like carbonated bath water. Sometimes I thought that it was very good that I could not get my hands on a steady supply of the Demon Drink, for after a long day of Roger and the lovely Mr Jamil, our former hospital director, I would probably have taken to the bottle with verve.

The dining-room food, if ghastly, was at least consistent. I once went to see the food service officer with a complaint from a patient and discovered that we had something called a Three-Week Rotating Menu. On further enquiry I found that their idea of a three-week rotating menu was nothing like mine. It did not mean that there were twenty-one days of different meals, but that you had the same meal for twenty-one days and then they changed the vegetable. For the Arabs the meat was mutton, whacked with a cleaver into unappealing lumps, bone and all, and then thoroughly boiled in its own fat. For the Asians, and Europeans, it was chicken par-boiled en masse in enormous steel cauldrons and then fried in olive oil; it was very greasy and tasted strange. The vegetable, for there was only ever one, was presented in a huge steel barrel. There was white rice for the Filipinos, yellow for the Arabs and one with a pinkish colour, probably from Dal, for the Indians. There was unleavened bread, a small plastic cup of plain camel's milk yoghurt, and one piece of fruit. The fruit also rotated every twenty-one days, so that we got three weeks of oranges, then apples, then pears. There was a cupful of something liquid in a plastic container that was alleged to be tea.

The diet was so incredibly boring that I could only think of having a big eat-up when I went out. At least there was no problem getting enough to eat, once I had the cook chatted up so that I could get two pieces of chicken in lieu of bread or rice. This took a while, but my unfailing charm and my love of food won out in the end. Wherever I have gone my first and foremost policy has always been to make friends with the cook.

25 Killer doctor

The fractured English I encountered every day was irresistibly funny. The hospital director and various directors of departments sent around circulars that were a glorious source of fractured English: the original would be in Arabic with an English translation on one side.

One epistle came addressed, 'Hallow My Collies.' I think he meant Hello, my colleagues, and not an exhortation to deify his dogs. Several came to me as Most Respected Madam.

Once a circular came around saying there would be a Muck Up of the hospital disaster plan. Another said that there would be a Mid-Nigh snack for the Mid-Nigh nurses. Another said nurses were not to run down doctors to get charts signed. Then there were the names of various staff members: Doctor Boozer, Doctor Budgie, Doctor Killy, Doctor Jabber, who really was the immunologist, Doctor Mucki, Doctor Fairies Toe and Doctor Munchie.

There were nurses named Marilyn Gum Bag, Immaculata Goo and Gin Sog, and an exquisitely beautiful and fragile Korean nurse who rejoiced in the positively awful handle of Oxen. Sam Sook was a theatre orderly; Abdul Basher worked in theatre. Mad Bonga worked in the nursing office. Mohommed Shed was one of the cleaners, and John Fat was a technician.

There was a cleaner called Mudler and another, a sweet little thing, called Nag.

The patients came tagged as Jawz Camel, Bugga Turkey, Hag Hamid, and so on.

In Egypt I found a book entitled *Travels in Egypt*, by O. Muck. Another book I found in the hospital library was called *Medical Science in Islam* and was written by Dr Ischmail Cut Cut.

There was a brand of chocolates sold in the compound shop called Bum Fest. Once I found a sign on a toilet provocatively inviting me to Push Bottom.

From one of the nurses I received an invitation to a birthday 'panty', from another a note explaining that she would do something 'as soon as quickly after they came', and from another a request for a 'wowser' for her travel tickets. No trouble to find one of those in Saudi. By Australian standards the place was crawling with them.

In the patients' notes a doctor wishing to transfer his patient to intensive care wrote that he was to be sent to the 'insensitive' care unit. I was the supervisor of it at the time and was not sure if I should be offended. But even this did not sound quite as bad as a place to which we sent patients in Medina, which was called, and I hope not descriptively, 'minimal care'. Then there was a place I often heard referred to as the 'sarcastic clinic' and which had me puzzled, until one day I followed someone to it and discovered it to be nothing more remarkable than the psychiatric clinic!

In our hospital we gave people 'cream' enemas instead of barium. (Scream enemas would have been better) and we restrained violent patients with 'depravure'.

Then there were the menus. I have always enjoyed reading menus in foreign countries, for even when the tucker was not too good I got a really good laugh out of the menu. I found some gems on Saudi menus, beginning with an 'oven-backed hammer' which, though it sounded tough on the tooth, turned out to be a kind of fish. Accompanying the hammer were 'battered vegetables', and 'mashrooms' – the hammers had been at them too. The alternative offering was 'steak graniture', which could be accomplished by a 'sliced green'.

I also added to my list a few quaint ironies. The vending machine in the hospital foyer had an attendant seated alongside it. No-one would have been able to use it without help, and the Bedu would have punched it to death if it took their money and did not produce the goods.

Traffic lights and stop signs often had police guards. Nobody would have stopped otherwise and some still did not. And finally by a wonderful accident of fate, the doorbell of the maternity ward of the hospital up the road played Happy Birthday.

26 Good morning, Sir

The hospital was now a familiar place and I felt a part of it. As the director of nursing I was accorded some measure of respect. The Pakistani security guards leapt to attention as I passed on my rounds, and saluting me said, 'Good morning, Sir.' Here the men saluted me and the women kissed me.

I had been getting on with my job as best I could and enjoyed my work. Making progress, however slight, was rewarding. Time, which had stood still in the beginning, now passed more quickly and, towards the end of July, we entered *Dul Haja*, the time of the pilgrimage.

During this month, over two million of the faithful from all over the world come to visit the holy places of Mecca and Medina, and many Saudis also make the journey. A pilgrimage can be made at any time, but this is the time of greatest religious significance, because the flight of the prophet took place at this time. *Haj* lasts for the entire month, with *Idl Adha*, the festival of sacrifice (when most people sacrifice an animal) coming on the tenth day.

I had been told horror stories of the chaos that came with the *Haj*, when the hospital was filled to bursting with pilgrims, who became ill or were injured in car accidents or brawls and riots among rival Muslim sects. The *Haj* is at the hottest time of the year and pilgrims must walk a long way in the sun between shrines wearing only the *Imhram* and with uncovered heads.

At the beginning of the *Haj* there was a shortage of a hundred and fifty nurses and we were expecting a tenfold increase in our workload. At the end of the month we had seen over twelve thousand patients in casualty. Many deaths occurred and the carnage on the roads was unbelievable. There was an almost constant stream of Red Crescent ambulances (the Arab equivalent of the Red Cross, using a crescent moon, one of the symbols of Islam, instead of the Christian cross) pulling up at the doors. I used to plead daily with the hospital director for more nurses, but all I ever got were promises. I was even given the numbers who were supposedly on their way – twenty, thirty, once even a hundred, which was somewhere near the number we needed. A small trickle of staff came but not enough to replace those who left when their contracts finished. When I came to the hospital there were one hundred and forty-three female Koreans, but thirty-four left in one month as their contracts expired. Their salaries had been cut and they could get almost as much money in Korea, where the conditions were better. They were less submissive women than the other Asians, less tolerant of the restrictions and better trained than most of the other nurses. I was sorry to see them go. The Saudis had begun to realise that the oil revenue was drying up. They had been outrageously diddled in the beginning because of their lack of worldliness and had wasted enormous amounts of money. Then Opec dropped the price of oil and they had to economise. Before this they had either had no money at all, so it did not matter, or they had so much that it was no object. They had no idea where or how to start economising and did all the wrong things, such as cutting nurses' wages and reducing essential supplies. Then they could not understand why their hospitals were not efficient. They should have increased the salaries, rather than decreased them, so that they could have attracted better qualified staff. The best Asian nurses who wanted to work overseas went to America or the UK. The Ministry of Health could not see this.

When the *Haj* started, the director's solution was to order that none of the nurses should have a day off for the entire month. He said that I could give them the time off after the *Haj*. We both knew that this was impossible. So did the nurses who were still waiting for their time off from last year. I pleaded with the hospital director in vain.

Company staff were also penalised, although they could not make us work without a day off. They probably would have ignored our contracts and tried to do so, if not for the fact that the company had its administrator on site. Nevertheless we still had to work far in excess of our regular hours.

We were also confined to the compound. The company refused to let us travel on the road during the *Haj*, so trips out stopped. The company bus had only just started its Friday outings again after its mishap with the donkey. Now it was grounded again. But it was madness to venture out on the roads during the *Haj*.

The mayhem on the roads defied description. There are few road rules in Saudi Arabia and anyone can get a licence to drive. Anyone who has the money to put on the counter to buy a licence can do so, no matter how young, or old, or decrepit, or blind. The only thing which deters you from getting a licence and driving a car is being female. There is no driving test or age limit, and the fashion is for large, powerful modern cars. As the price of fuel does not matter, the attitude is the bigger the better. Little boys of ten years old drive about in whacking great cars. In the male orthopædic ward about this time, there was a room of eight beds full of little boys from the one accident. The oldest was nine years old and he was the driver of the car in which they had their accident. None of them was badly hurt; they were mostly suffering from cuts and bruises, all with a few stitches somewhere on their faces and heads. Two days later they had got over their initial fright and were jumping around from bed to bed, looking cheeky, grinning happily and greatly interested in this new experience. No-one was the least perturbed or concerned that the driver was only nine years old. Instead they seemed to be rather amused by the incident.

Seat belts are not worn. There were five-minute programmes on the television every evening aimed at improving road safety. At home they would have been a colossal insult to the intelligence. For example, there was one which began with a picture of a stop sign and continued, 'This is a stop sign. When you see this sign you must stop your car. Before the sign, not after it. Then you must look to be sure that there is no-one coming before you move off again.' Countless Saudis did not know what a stop sign was. I often saw them ignored by drivers when we were out in the bus.

Another advertisement went, 'The white lines are traffic lines. They are put there to show you where to drive on the road. You must only go one way in a lane.' If that sounds funny, I have seen them going the wrong way in a built up area of Jeddah against a cavalry charge of traffic. Many Saudis do not know what the white lines on the road are for.

The slaughter on the roads started on the first day of the *Haj* with a shocking two-bus smash that left twenty dead. The survivors made casualty look like a battlefield. There were torn and blood-stained bodies everywhere. Twenty-nine were admitted to the wards. The worst accidents happened on the road between Mecca and Medina. This was the path the *Haj* took, formerly on foot or by camel. Now this road was traversed by buses and cars. The buses were impossibly overcrowded, the driver's sole aim being to get there as fast as possible, with as many people as possible, and then go back for another load. With the philosophy that Allah will take over in an emergency, the driver travelled as fast as the gas pedal would allow him.

Our water in the quarters was now rationed. It was cut off from five in the morning, after the faithful had performed their ritual ablutions before the dawn prayer, until they needed it again for their evening prayer washing, at about half past eight. The water was diverted to the Guests of God. Thousands of them were living camped on the plains close to the hospital. The way they lived and the facilities available were extremely primitive. Although the king gave regular allowances for the upkeep of the camps, there were many instances of disease, and epidemics of varying severity were usual. This year there were outbreaks of cholera and meningitis, and an entire floor of the hospital had to be allocated to isolate both the meningitis and the cholera cases.

The first time the water was cut off without warning I was caught waterless. After that, every night I took to filling the bath, two buckets and a couple of plastic drums I had acquired from a friendly soul in the pharmacy. I used to do the washing by filling the machine manually, not recommended for speed or comfort, but quite effective, and took a cold morning splash bath in the manner of the Malaysian *mandi*.

During the *Haj* the post office did not even pretend to open as it had in *Ramadan*. A postal service could not continue between Jeddah and Medina, with the chaos the extra million or more visitors made of flight times. Consequently there was a whole month without letters from family and friends. I found the isolation hard. My mother always wrote to me every Sunday on the distinctive Australian aerogrammes, which by now were recognisable to all of the nursing and company staff. The two large, cheery Egyptian secretaries who staffed the nursing office and who were always addressed as Madame Yasmin and Madame Zenobia when using their names, but Sister when not, would say to me, 'Here is your mother's letter for this week, Sister Lydia.'

A lot of mail was lost at times because the Saudi hospital Postal Pixie, whom I named The Poison Dwarf, could not read or write English. If he could not decipher the name on the letter, it would go anywhere, or into the bin, if he was feeling particularly poisonous. At mail time someone from the company would appear to mount guard over him and salvage what he mis-sorted. A system evolved in which mail was sent out of the country with anyone going on leave to Europe or the UK. This my nephew dubbed, 'Nurse Mail', and the title stuck. It was far safer than the Saudi mail, which ran the gauntlet of possible mishaps and incompetence before it got safely out of the country, not the least of which was the censor. Nurse Mail was also subject to censorship if confiscated at customs but was usually much safer. The people in customs were generally far too busy looking for dirty pictures, and books about Jews, which they were positive we all had a penchant for.

I recorded my diary, from which this book is written, on cassette tapes, and then sent them out by Nurse Mail, taping the call to prayer and some of the Arabic lessons from the television at the beginning, hoping that this would confuse the censor. I figured he would be bored to sleep by the time he got to the messages home and my diary. You just never knew what the censor might find offensive, and I did not want to risk being caught with tapes or a diary in my baggage when I left the country. I would not have been allowed to write diaries: if they had thought that I was collecting material for a book, or found notebooks in my room, I would have been deported or put in prison. Even so I was very nervous when the time came to go out through customs.

27 The great camel race

The end of my contract loomed. With the leave owing to me, I should have been due to finish in early August, but my request for an exit visa was refused. The director said I could not go during the *Haj* because, as director of nursing, I was needed. His word was law. It would have been madness to try to travel at this time anyway. All the local flights to and from Riyadh, Medina or Jeddah had been booked for months by pilgrims. Even after getting on an international flight list, there was the possibility of being bumped off to give precedence to a pilgrim going home.

I submitted without too much disappointment. Already I was brainwashed to accept that I would leave when they wished it.

Great news came half way through the *Haj*. There were ten nurses being sent to work at KFH from the now defunct eye hospital in Medina. They were all Egyptian women recruited for an MOH-run hospital. Now I saw the Arab idea of a nurse. Ten of them crowded into my office. They were wearing the most motley arrangement of clothing and footwear outside of a Bad Taste Party: highheeled gold dancing shoes, black ankle strap sandals, fake lizard skin coats, plastic scuffs, blue velvet bedroom slippers with fluffy rabbit fur trim. One wore a wedding dress. The rest were in a selection of white and once white gowns, caftans, and floor-length robes. The wedding dress trailed along the ground. They were bundled up in various coloured shawls and woollies against the airconditioning. I could see why the eye hospital was now declared to be defunct. My joy evaporated. I had doubts about their efficiency and was worried when I dispatched them to the wards. They proved, to a woman, to be hopeless. Their training did not seem to be that of a cleaner. They could not answer the simplest question on basic nursing care and had no idea about asepsis, treatments, or drugs.

In the end, having given them instruction on what was an acceptable standard of dress for KFH, and seeing they were issued with MOH uniforms (most of them had the correct figure to fill them admirably), I banished them to the depths of the outpatients clinics where, under the eye of the excellent Filipino charge nurse, I hoped they could do no harm. She occasionally complained to me about them piteously, but my heart was made of stone. I did not want them on the wards.

In the second week of the *Haj*, the Saudis had the feast of *Idl Adha*. We serfs of the Saudis did not. During the feast time I watched the famous king's camel races on television, a meeting for all the thousands of Bedu from the desert, who set up camp and take part. The races started from a huge stadium before the king and lots of royalty (but no women). There were about one thousand camels in each race, and there were four races; one for lightcoloured camels, one for dark, one for old and one for young, but there was no other handicapping system. It made an impressive spectacle, this great multitude of camels galloping off, riders on their humps wielding camel sticks, at great speed over the plains.

Somehow we all survived to the end of the *Haj*. The

company had sent none of the masses of nursing staff they had constantly promised. When I had long since given up, two actually did arrive. One man lasted three months, went on leave and was never heard of again: the other was a complete fool whom I also had to hide in outpatients. This was not difficult, for I never saw such a rabbit warren of a place.

After the *Haj* was over and the moon was once again decreed to be in the correct phase, the new year was announced. It was 1409 and felt it: terribly mediæval.

28 Freedom

My time was up, the *Haj* was over and the director and the company still persisted in trying to convince me to renew my contract. I had not yet received the money I was owed in salary increases. The company intimated that I would get it, and a large increase when I renewed it. It looked like I was being blackmailed, so I decided to fight fire with fire. I signed a new contract to return to Saudi Arabia as a director of nursing for another year, but stipulated that I was to receive a transfer from KFH. I might have been imprisoned there for a year because of my ignorance in the beginning, but I would never have considered returning. Then I submitted an application for holiday leave, which was granted immediately. It was as I thought: they had been holding me to ransom. I had no wish to stay any longer. It had been a personal triumph to last the distance and survive the appalling social and emotional deprivation in Medina. I was only the third company person to finish a contract at KFH, and I doubted that there would be many more. I thought the company's contract to manage the hospital would not last long.

With my leave granted and my exit visa approved, I set about making plans to go home. It was now over six months since my leave in Egypt. This time I wanted to go home to Australia. I could not wait to live again –

and with normal people (well, almost normal). The one thing I was longing to see, after the obligatory long tall glass of sinfulness, was rain. I had seen no rain, except for the ten spots that fell when the king was in residence, in a whole year.

Winter would not be quite finished at home yet and I even wanted to be cold. I wrote and asked my long-suffering family to send me a picture of a man. My memory of them was hazy and I did not want to make any embarrassing mistakes. Where I was they were the ones in the long dresses while we women wore the trousers.

I had a letter from my recruiters, offering me the choice of two posts, one in Damman and one in Riyadh, both with the Ministry of Defence, who are the best people to work for in Saudi Arabia. Damman is by far the most liberal place towards westerners.

Preparing to leave I sold off, or gave away to the cleaners and other needy persons, my surplus gear and packed my neglected jodphurs, riding boots and other essentials.

The great day of my liberation dawned and I was escorted to the airport, to be sent on my way to Singapore through Riyadh by two company officials. It was their job to see me safely on the plane and out of the country in case I went astray, or decided I could not bear to leave all this good life. I had to step over the line into that part of the departure lounge from which there is no return before I could reach back and take my passport from them. How good it felt to hold it in my hand again, making me once more, like the Bedu, master of my own destiny.

The company administrator, Paul Sharp, had handed me a reference as I said goodbye to him, and I read it now with pleasure as I sat in the departure lounge. He wrote that I had dramatically improved the morale of the staff and their working conditions, as well as raising the standard of nursing care. No greater compliment can be paid to a nurse in a managerial position.

The flight was announced. I went out on to the tarmac with the crowd. Clutching my passport and heaving a sigh of relief, I walked straight and fast, controlling an urge to run, towards the waiting Saudi plane and home.

Wakefield Press

MONSTER LOVE
Jeri Kroll

I hate you, I love you, I hate you, I love you. That's clear unambiguous truth. . .

Jeri Kroll's third collection of poems is a passionate and witty excursion into the world of the family. She writes about pregnancy, the growing independence of the child and the difficulties of raising other people's children. As well, she investigates wider issues, such as jealousy, divorce and the shifting images women have of themselves.

'Here the universal is made personal and the personal made universal and that, truly, is how literature at its best mirrors and deepens our lives for us.'

Kate Llewellyn

'The best poems in *Monster Love* are in fact worth many times the price of the whole book; as a gift for the thinking novice, or even experienced mum, Kroll's offering might be genuinely treasured.'

The Sunday Telegraph

ISBN 1 86254 265 1   RRP $10.95

Wakefield Press

Geoff Goodfellow's Poetry Trifecta

NO TICKET NO START

'These are powerful, abrasive, compassionate poems that give building workers an authentic voice not heard so clearly since the Green Ban days.'

Caroline Jones, *ABC Radio*
The Search for Meaning

ISBN 1 86254 264 3   RRP $5.95

NO COLLARS NO CUFFS

'This is poetry that means business . . . Goodfellow is proof that people will buy poetry, and will laugh and cry and ask for more.'

Kevin Brophy, *Australian Book Review*

Now in its seventh printing, *No Collars No Cuffs* continues to enjoy enormous popularity throughout the nation.

ISBN 0 949363 07 3   RRP $9.95

BOW TIE & TAILS

'Geoff Goodfellow . . . pushes poetry as something real, living, using the language of the heart and the street, the voice of battlers and the beaten, those who make it by the skin of their teeth, and those who don't.'

Carol Treloar, *The Advertiser*

ISBN 0 86254 996 6   RRP $12.95

Wakefield Press

BLACK HORSE ODYSSEY
David Harris

Out of the Gobi Desert comes a wonderful book. Reading it, we go on the adventure of a lifetime — the quest for a lost city called Rome.

For centuries the existence of Li-jien, a city the ancient Chinese called Rome, was a mystery to scholars. Then, in early March 1988, David Harris received copies of the life's work of a former professor of Chinese history at Oxford University. The evidence was too powerful to ignore. Amateur, obsessed, alone, Harris set out on an ordinary man's journey of extraordinary discovery.

Married beside the Yellow River, swept up in the murderous events of the Tiananmen massacre, Harris records day by day the exciting steps he took on his travels into the unknown.

Part history, part adventure, *Black Horse Odyssey* is much more than a fascinating collection of stories. The site David Harris identified on 7 May 1989 has since been declared a National Monument of China and is now a focus of international academic research. As this edition goes to print, fierce controversy brings to light incredible new facts about the city built by Romans 1,300 years before Marco Polo entered Cathay. Illustrations, maps and photographs illuminate the journal entries as we witness history in the remaking.

ISBN 1 86254 270 8   To be released October 1991

Wakefield Press

THE LONG WAY HOME
'Nobody Goes That Way'
Lydia Laube

Lydie Laube returns to Saudi Arabia, collects her pay, and decides to take *The Long Way Home* through Egypt, Sudan, Kenya and India. Our Good Little Woman is as eccentric and entertaining as ever ... blithely she trots along, sunshade held aloft, while behind her ships sink, hotels explode and wars erupt.

ISBN 1 86254 325 9   RRP $14.95